Constantin Brancusi
1876–1957
A Retrospective Exhibition

BY SIDNEY GEIST

THE SOLOMON R. GUGGENHEIM MUSEUM, NEW YORK

IN COLLABORATION WITH

PHILADELPHIA MUSEUM OF ART

THE ART INSTITUTE OF CHICAGO

Published by The Solomon R. Guggenheim Foundation, New York, 1969
Library of Congress Card Catalogue Number: 76-95574
All Rights Reserved, Printed in Austria

LENDERS

Mr. and Mrs. James W. Alsdorf, Winnetka, Illinois
Mr. and Mrs. Lee A. Ault, New York
Mr. and Mrs. Lester Francis Avnet, New York
Miss Kathi Baer
Mr. and Mrs. Isidore Cohen, New York
Mr. and Mrs. Ralph F. Colin, New York
Mr. and Mrs. John Cowles, Minneapolis
Richard S. Davis, New York
Mr. and Mrs. Harold Diamond, New York
Mr. and Mrs. Malcolm Eisenberg, Philadelphia
Mrs. Stanca Fotino-Morar, Bucharest
Peggy Guggenheim Foundation, Venice
Joseph H. Hirshhorn Collection, New York
R. Sturgis Ingersoll, Penllyn, Pennsylvania
Mrs. Howard M. Kinney, Washington, D.C.
Mrs. H. Gates Lloyd, Haverford, Pennsylvania
Mrs. Barnett Malbin, Birmingham, Michigan
Collection George Oprescu, Bucharest
Mrs. Yolanda Penteado, São Paulo
Joseph Pulitzer, Jr., St. Louis
Mr. and Mrs. Herbert M. Rothschild, Ossining, New York
Mr. and Mrs. Adolf Schaap, Philadelphia
Mrs. Mary Sisler, Palm Beach
Mr. and Mrs. Frederick Stafford, New York
Miss Kate Rodina Steichen, Wilton, Connecticut
Mrs. George H. Warren, New York
Mrs. Benjamin P. Watson, Danbury, Connecticut
Mrs. John Wintersteen, Philadelphia
Private collection, New York

Museum of Fine Arts, Boston
Muzeul de Arta R. S. R., Bucharest
Albright-Knox Art Gallery, Buffalo
Fogg Art Museum, Harvard University, Cambridge,
    Massachusetts
The Arts Club of Chicago
The Art Institute of Chicago
Cleveland Museum of Art, Ohio
Muzeul de Arta, Craiova
Norton Simon Museum of Art, Inc., Fullerton, California
The Museum of Fine Arts, Houston
University of Nebraska Art Galleries, Lincoln
The J. B. Speed Art Museum, Louisville
The Metropolitan Museum of Art, New York
The Solomon R. Guggenheim Museum, New York
Portland Art Museum, Oregon
Musée National d'Art Moderne, Paris
Philadelphia Museum of Art

Sidney Janis Gallery, New York

INTRODUCTION

Although Constantin Brancusi's name stands in pure splendor among those who have given form and meaning to modern art, his achievement reaches us ordinarily through single sculptures, while exhibitions of his work are rare. Through their perfection, rarity, uniqueness, and through their value Brancusi's sculptures are, in the real sense of the word, treasures—treasures guarded in relative isolation from one another and seldom allowed to combine in even temporary interaction. To interrupt the remoteness of single works and to give a sense of Brancusi's total sculptural oeuvre is the purpose of this exhibition—an ambitious undertaking initiated by The Solomon R. Guggenheim Museum in close cooperation with the Philadelphia Museum of Art and The Art Institute of Chicago.

The task of developing the exhibition concept and preparing first an ideal, and eventually a possible, exhibition plan, devolved upon Sidney Geist, whose recent monograph, *Brancusi* (Grossman Publishers, New York, 1968), constituted an extraordinary qualification for such an assignment. Following his appointment as Guest Curator of the Exhibition in 1968, Mr. Geist, with the support of Dr. Louise Averill Svendsen, Curator of The Solomon R. Guggenheim Museum, and of her staff, worked to produce the current exhibition and the accompanying catalogue. The sponsoring museums are, therefore, much in his debt.

Brancusi's artistic legacy is concentrated in a relatively few collections. Museums owning a sizeable group of Brancusi's works are: the Musée National d'Art Moderne in Paris, to whom the artist bequeathed the works found in his atelier upon his death; the Philadelphia Museum of Art, which particularly through the Arensberg Collection has come to own a splendid assemblage of Brancusi's in all media; and, in New York City, the Museum of Modern Art and The Solomon R. Guggenheim Museum have each acquired important Brancusi collections. In addition to these, only the Rumanian Museums in Bucharest and in Craiova are in possession of more than a very few important works. It has greatly aided the organization of this retrospective that almost all of these institutions have lent in significant numbers and that such loans were further enriched by museums with small Brancusi holdings, as well as through private loans obtained from sources throughout the world. As a result of such participation the exhibition of 84 sculptures and 23 drawings, while still incomplete and inevitably vulnerable in its effort to represent fully all of Brancusi's motifs, fulfills the expectations of the organizers through a selection that is more continuous and comprehensive than any previous one. This is due of course to the generosity of all lenders to whom, in behalf of the participating museums and that of the exhibition's guest curator, I express our deep gratitude.

In behalf of the Guggenheim Museum I would like to express thanks to the Directors of the collaborating Museums—Dr. Evan H. Turner and Charles C. Cunningham who, with the help of their staffs, have been in effective attendance through many crucial stages of the exhibition's development. Equally important were the contributions of M. Jean Chatelain, Directeur des Musées de France, M. Jean Leymarie, Conservateur en Chef of the Musée National d'Art Moderne, Mme. Denise Roché, Dr. P. Atanasiu who, together with Dr. L. J. F. Wijsenbeek, Director of the Gemeentemuseum in The Hague, have given much valuable advice, both scholarly and technical, through which the exhibition, as well as the documentation in the following catalogue pages, has been importantly enriched.

In Brancusi's native Rumania, M. Vasile Florea, Directeur of the State Committee on Visual Arts, and the Directors of the Museums in Bucharest and in Craiova, as well as, Mr. Mircea Popescu, Mr. Barbu Brezianu and others have been instrumental in furthering this project and in contributing, besides important loans, scholarly information of consequence.

It remains to acknowledge the valuable intermediary services rendered in Washington, D. C. by Messrs. Frank Shakespeare, Director of the United States Information Agency, Pic Littell and Kempton B. Jenkins, successive Assistant Directors of the Soviet Union and Eastern European Department of that organization, and Nicolae Atanasiu, First Secretary, Rumanian Embassy, and to Mr. Harry G. Barnes Jr., and Mr. Daniel J. Hafrey, respectively Chargé d'Affaires and First Secretary for Press and Culture, United States Embassy in Bucharest.

Thomas M. Messer, Director
The Solomon R. Guggenheim Museum

Constantin Brancusi

The sculpture of Brancusi presents a universe of form where all is clear and filled with light. All, at the level of *form*, is given and given at once, without reserve, without mystery or surprise. Form in this sculpture is, in the simple sense of the word, revealed, innocently and nakedly.

Enigmatic in only rare instances, Brancusi's *imagery* is for the most part as manifest as form itself. Here are heads, bodies, birds and animals, seen with child-like simplicity unencumbered by attributes, uninfected by irony or arrière-pensée. Joy, health and a sense of high play are the primary characteristics of this art, and emanate from it as they must have done from the first creatures on the first day.

Yet, in spite of the frankness of Brancusi's offering, we often read riddles in the sculpture, and for a number of reasons. "Modern art," with its general intransigence, shock tactics and intellectuality, has made us wary of being taken in. The sculptor's deep innocence is not ours, and is suspect therefore. Then too, the very nature of Brancusi's art, its quality of being stripped bare, attracts a host of ambiguities—inevitably, since the magic of sheer form and the effectiveness of an image belong to the realm of the ineffable. But probably the chief source of difficulty is the fact that in most cases knowledge of the sculpture is fragmentary. As a result it has become customary to take any available or much published object as the quintessence of the work. It has even become customary to raise lofty critical structures on a foundation of photographs.

The occasion of a large exhibition ought to correct this situation. It ought to demonstrate that the Brancusi of *Endless Column*, or of *Bird in Space*, or of *The Kiss* or of *The Turtle*, is the Brancusi of all of these and of much more; that beneath the variety of outward manifestation there is a constant body of thought and feeling. It should warn us of the error of taking any part for the whole; it may even make clear that there is a whole here that needs all its parts.

Since we now have a larger view of the work than ever before, it will be useful to take account of it in a direct fashion. We shall aim as studiously as possible to see what is there, and postpone for as long as possible our assault on the ineffable.

Considered as a whole, the sculpture of Brancusi presents several distinct features.

First, while seeming to show great diversity of theme, construction, size and purpose, the body of work is not large. The extant works—not counting plaster casts of objects in stone, wood and bronze—may be numbered at slightly over two hundred; as far as we can tell, some fifty other works may be counted as lost, destroyed and kept from public attention. Then there are a number of stools, benches and doorways, the many pedestals, and the far from numerous drawings and paintings. All this is the production of a period of activity just over a half century in length, from 1898 to 1949.

Second, the work is easily divisible into two clearly marked phases: the student and early works up to the Stanescu monument, and the mature period beginning at that point, 1907, and manifesting an individuality not evident earlier. In spite of the sharp difference between these phases in matters of construction and intention, the later work, as we shall see, reflects the thematic concerns and basic sensibility of the earlier.

Third, the mature phase seems to present an unwavering vision, a formal approach so constant that many observers have been led to think that Brancusi, once he had found his path, stopped developing. This impression no doubt arises from the large form and the smooth surface so often to be seen in the sculpture. But behind these pervasive and obvious features lies a great variety of construction; each new theme calls forth a new formal and expressive situation. At the same time certain themes are pursued in later versions because they have an importance not exhausted in the first effort. Brancusi's interweaving of fresh ventures and of themes already broached creates a model of artistic endeavor which puts in question our usual notions concerning originality and invention.

The fourth feature of the oeuvre is one which makes it easy to consider it as a whole; the clarity of its physical outlines. Brancusi's studio was not cluttered by the sketches, starts, and unfinished projects common to most sculptor's studios. Besides the finished works, there is a scored and abandoned marble head of a child; a *Bird in Space* in the initial stages being roughed out; two studies in plaster, a bust and a figure, made some forty years earlier, and a rough plaster head very much like *The First Cry* that had never, it seems, been realized. In all, an amazingly small number of unfulfilled beginnings, if that is what they all were, after the labors of half a century. We do not know how many unachieved works were destroyed by the sculptor, but the oeuvre that he left us gives the impression of having no loose ends, no gropings in many directions, no ultimate frustrations. Here is a body of work whose limits appear to be perfectly contained by the artist. Enviable in its scope, dazzling in its perfections, tentative only in its repetitions, the scale of this effort is human rather than superhuman. No image here of the artist producing indiscriminately, in vegetable abundance, or devouring all past and all possible styles. Brancusi's oeuvre, in short, does not overwhelm us; it is governed by the same intelligence that informs the separate works, by the same clarity, reserve and purposefulness, the same absence of the "grandiloquent" and the "monumental," to use his own words.

Up to the time of the Stanescu monument Brancusi was outstandingly a portraitist; he studied the cast and worked from life and from photographs; he made excellent portraits (and eventually with speed) at school, on commission, and for his own purposes. He had, to be sure, studied the figure and made a life-sized *écorché* in Rumania, but he was dissatisfied with his figure studies at the Ecole des Beaux-Arts in Paris, and seems to have saved none of them. In his mature period, though the veridical portrait held no interest for him, his attention to the theme of the human head was undiminished, and resulted in works whose number far exceeds that devoted to any other theme. Seventy-nine sculptures, or forty-two percent of the 190 extant works made after *The Prayer*, 1907, are heads and busts; of these, twenty-three are of children. Pursuing these statistics we observe that there are thirty-six other human images; twenty-seven *Birds* and twenty-three other representations of animals that together constitute more than a quarter of the extant mature oeuvre; nineteen architectural images, nine objects, and *Exotic Plant*. These numbers are a sure sign of a hierarchy of thematic value, though it should be noted that human subjects predominate at the beginning of the oeuvre and animal subjects at the end; *Exotic Plant* appears at a point past the middle. Brancusi's animal themes include: bird, fish, penguin, cock, seal, turtle, and a "nocturnal animal." Among humans the female is favored over the male: "Nude men in sculpture," he said, "are not as beautiful as toads." Finally, images of children constitute a sixth of the extant oeuvre. Brancusi's statement, "When we are no longer like children we are already dead," is no pious or merely period utterance.

Except for a very few pieces—*Torment*, where a boy winces in pain, *Portrait of Nicolae Dărăscu* in which the young painter is caught with his arm raised before a canvas (both of which precede *The Prayer*), and *The Prayer* itself, which portrays a kneeling woman in the act of crossing herself—by far the preponderant number of Brancusi's human images shows man in a quiescent state, indeed often sleeping. Even *The Kiss*, a theme taken up many times by the sculptor. seems to portray a state of being rather than action, more energy emanating from the lovers' glance than from the embracing figures. Stillness is not absolute, however: though fixed, *Narcissus* stares; the *Sleeping Muse* is tremulous in sleep; the *Torso of a Young Man* is alert, the *Torso of a Girl* held in precarious balance.

Action in Brancusi's sculpture is assigned to the animal images. The *Bird* speaks, calls to the sky or sweeps through space; the *Cock* crows; the *Fish* flashes; the *Turtle* wallows or "flies"; the muscular *Seal* stretches. Action, in its turn, is restrained, and depicted only in the first *Bird* and *Turtle*, for the rest the images are infused with the suggestion of energy by the sculptor's art rather than by signs of effort.

In the later work, except for one version of *The Kiss* and *Wisdom of the Earth*, man is never depicted whole; except for the *Penguins*, animals are never shown other than whole. It would seem that in the Brancusian view man is fragmented —when not in love; animals in their wholeness are free to act— the *Penguins* are merely huddled together, like people.

The greater mass of the oeuvre is comprised of pleasing images: innocent children, alert youths, beautiful women, and energetic members of the animal kingdom; love, beauty, sheer joy are the motivating forces here. But we note a surprising number of troubled images. *Torment* shows a boy being beaten; *The New-born* evokes the shock of birth; *Prometheus* touches the theme of general human suffering in the shape of a child's head; another child's head, lost, is a study of a pathological type. We note the grotesques of *Double Caryatid*, the disturbing *Chimera*, the threatening *King of Kings*, the less than pleasant *Nocturnal Animal*.

If *The Kiss* is a portrayal of erotic love, *Adam and Eve* comments of the non-amatory relations of the male and the female. In *The Redskins* the sculptor deplores the fate of the American Indian; *Boundary Marker* refers us to the sphere of politics; *King of Kings* was intended to allude to Eastern mysticism, as its original title, *Spirit of Buddha*, tells us. *The Chief* and *Portrait of Nancy Cunard* are social commentaries. *Leda* is a metamorphic creature: womanbird. *Cup* and *Vase* are celebrations of commonplace objects. The range of the sculptor's explicit reference is uncommonly wide, and several works clearly have metaphysical significance. *Bird in Space* is an image of transcendance; *The Turtle*, of earth-hugging persistence. *Endless Column* is, in its first appearance, a handsome decoration in human proportions; the taller version in Edward Steichen's garden seemed like the shape of human thought in a natural world; the final ninety-six foot column, the third element in the ensemble at Tirgu Jiu, is the climactic motif in a sculptural meditation on human destiny and eternity.

Impressive as this catalogue may be, Brancusi's thought insinuates itself only gradually on the attention, and is hinted at in an occasional catalogue note or suggestive title: *Beginning of the World*. Nor is he unremittingly serious; high play and humor are evident everywhere, and clearly humorous notes are struck in *The Newborn*, *Little French Girl*, *The Chief* and the *Nancy Cunard*.

Brancusi has no recourse to symbols or symbolism. He distills thought in the very process in which he concentrates form. "Simplicity is not an end in art," he said, "but we arrive at simplicity in spite of ourselves, as we approach the true sense of things."

The characteristic unity of a sculpture by Brancusi is not that of its formalist reputation, but rather a poetic unity in which thought and form are inseparable. Though these have been separated here for the sake of discussion, the one does not support, precede or contain the other; their congruence in the sculpture is perfect. Refined, rigorous and esthetical as Brancusi's art may be, he is attentive to a large world which he engages with humor and his own rare sweetness.

a.

By what seems to have been a tremendous effort of will and imagination, Brancusi abandons his studious realism in 1907 and begins to develop a vision of form that will remain constant for over forty years. He rationalizes the images which the world presents to him, and at the same time rationalizes the sculptural labor. The process is not merely stylistic in its effects, resulting in smoothing of surfaces, erasure of detail and simplification of shape. It is rather a way of thinking the forms of the world into new structures, structures not those of nature, *sculptural structures* which are at once a version of the external world and the shape of the sculptor's thought.

b.

Continuous as the Brancusian universe may appear, one structure does not suppose any other. *The Kiss* of Montparnasse (a) shows two embracing lovers; it does not supply the design for later male and female images. In the *Torso of a Young Man* (b) the legs are separated, and the resulting structure is forked at the bottom and phallic in appearance. In *Torso of a Young Woman* (c) the legs are together; by distillation in three ensuing versions, this massive design becomes a round-bottomed womb-like container. The slender *Bird in Space* leans back to face the sky in a euphoria of elevation; the heavy-bottomed *Cock*, tied to the earth despite its upward thrust, leans forward. Brancusi's analysis does not merely simplify the natural creature; it gives meaning to form. In the alternations of form we read a graphic language.

c.

Only rarely is Brancusi content with a unique expression: he has favored themes which he pursues in series. These series move toward different ends, so that in taking up again a compelling motif he does not necessarily work toward its perfection or greater abstraction, as is the case with *White Negress* or *Mlle. Pogany*. The Cock, for example, goes from a small and intimate state to a monumental, public one. The first version of *The Kiss*, personal in its significance and sensitive in its execution, in time becomes a generalized image rather mechanically rendered. The series of the *Birds* makes its way from a stylized representation with mythological reference to an image of spiritual flight. *Sleeping Muse*, a virtual portrait, initiates a series that moves from a representation of personal sleep to a vision of universal sleep: *Beginning of the World*. Cup, in its four versions, is an exploration of formal possibilities.

Working in series frees Brancusi from the demands of constant invention and gives his work a unity and continuity not at all at odds with its diversity. But there are themes with troublesome

d.

e.

demands, themes in which the sculptor takes leave of the specific and aims to pin down the absolute. The absolute is curiously undefinitive: Brancusi must make three versions of an absolute torso of a young man.

One of the chief keys to the understanding of Brancusi's mature oeuvre is his treatment of the sculpture as an object. The formal sign of this situation is the actual separation of the sculptured form from a base or device that would hold it in position. This is the case of course with those sculptures which are clearly objects, which are not fixed to bases, which may lie upon almost anything, and which may be handled: *Sleeping Muse*, the heads of sleeping children, *Prometheus*, the versions of *Cup*, *Vase*, and *Sculpture for the Blind/Beginning of the World*. But it is the case with all the other sculptures too. The significance of the sculpture/base relation becomes especially clear when we compare *The Kiss* by Rodin (d) and *The Kiss* (e) by Brancusi. In the Frenchman's sculpture the lovers, the rock they rest on, and the ground below both, are all actually continuous with each other; the ground serving as a base and the rock ambiguously so. In *The Kiss* by Brancusi, whether the full figures in the Cimetière Montparnasse or the half-figures to be seen in five other versions, the limit of the figures is the limit of the sculpture; the figures are not integral with a base or other device of any kind.

The sculptures created by both Rodin and Brancusi are discrete objects, as indeed are most sculptures. But Rodin's work images elements besides the bodies of the lovers, elements which create the illusion of a situation and a space in which the lovers find themselves. In Brancusi's carving we see only the lovers; they are set in real space, since they are congruent with the sculpture/object which is in real space.

The illusion of a situation in Rodin is perfectly consonant with the illusion of reality in the figures; in the case of Brancusi, the stylized figures make a *design* which very properly exists in real space. The difference in mode here becomes clear if we reverse the situation. If we remove the "ground" from the Rodin, there are those troublesome legs, and the sudden appearance of two shrunken humans in real space not to mention the rock, whose design would have to change and whose removal would alter everything. Similarly, we create a meaningless, indeed disastrous situation if we add a mass of stone below and integral with any version of *The Kiss* by Brancusi.

Rodin, Matisse, Duchamp-Villon, Archipenko and other sculptors of the early part of this century made sculptures which were integral with a base and others which were not. Of Brancusi we can say that no sculpture of the mature oeuvre—that is, from *The Prayer* on—is integral with a base. In the absoluteness of this distinction we must read a radical change in sensibility. Brancusi shuns illusion. He does not image space or a continuity of unlike things. His subjects become sculptured objects; they were indeed objects in the first place. His immediate sculptor's task is to make discrete bodies.

Rodin's *Prodigal Son*, ca. 1888, Bourdelle's *The Archer*, 1909 (f), Maillol's *Mediterranean*, 1902–05, Matisse's *The Slave*, 1900–03 (g), Duchamp-Villon's *Torso of a Young Man*, 1910, Archipenko's *Boxers*, 1914 (h),—all show figures continuous with a base, whether conventionally formal or more elaborately fashioned. On the other hand Brancusi's life-sized kneeling figure, *The Prayer*, terminates at its lower legs; the base is made of another material. *Caryatid* (p. 73) has no base at all. *Portrait of Mrs. Eugene Meyer, Jr.*, 1930, is in black marble, as are its base and pedestal, but the work is composed of three pieces of material. Here, as always, the sculpture is distinct from other objects, the sculptor's labor from the craftsman's, art from decoration.

Brancusi's avoidance of the base integral with a figure could not help but influence his choice of subjects and the form of his images. A modeled standing figure in the relatively normal proportions of *The Prayer*, and distinct from a base, would be in questionable taste. Images of figures dancing, on one leg, or at an unusual angle are of course ruled out. The *Caryatid*, one of the few standing works without a base, has large, heavy feet and, altogether, proportions not those of nature; *Little French Girl*, which stands on its own legs, is, like *Caryatid*, a highly stylized conception.

A special case of the avoidance of the base integral with the sculpture may be seen in Brancusi's treatment of the theme of the head. He sets a neck at an angle to the vertical head in both his first direct stone carving (lost) (i) and *Baroness R. F.* (j). The vertical neck of a head in the Apollinaire Collection (k) tapers almost to an edge, as does the curved neck of *Head of a Woman* in the collection of Mr. and Mrs. Isadore Levin, Detroit, (l). An early head, now lost, has no neck and is mounted on its chin. This is the case, too, of *White Negress* (m), and *Eileen* (n). The many heads of children, *Sleeping Muse* and *Prometheus* rest on their cheeks. The *Nancy Cunard* has a neck which is preternaturally thin. The neck of *The Chief* (o), is of normal size and on the same axis as the head, but the whole is tipped forward uniquely among Brancusi's works, and rests on a small plane. In short, Brancusi's treatment of the neck seems to be governed by an avoidance of a rounded, columnar, essentially neutral mass which he may well have considered as no more than a base below the focal head, as an inexpressive element he did not wish attached to the real object of his attention. Of the construction entitled *Portrait*, 1915, and exhibited as late as 1933, only the central portion now exists; it seems likely that the sculptor removed the lower portion because it too much resembled a base.

f.

g.

h.

i.

k.

l.

m.

n.

o.

If then, Brancusi makes a body which is not continuous with a base, that body in all but a few instances is not continuous with anything else. The exceptions make a short list: *The Kiss* and the *Penguins* show two or more creatures continuous with each other; arm and body are continuous in *Wisdom of the Earth, Portrait of George, A Muse, Mlle. Pogany* and *Princess X; Danaide* shows a serpentine earring along the left side of its neck; the three versions of *Maiastra* have the legs running along the body; and *White Negress* and the *Nancy Cunard* display an ornament and chignons. Only the last two of the sculptures originate after 1914, and they are a case in which the artist makes a point of the *addition* of forms, somewhat different from the contiguity of features that pertains in all the other instances. In the case of *The Chief* the crown or mitre is, of course, metal and not continuous with the wood of the carving.

Except for *Wisdom of the Earth, The Kiss* of Montparnasse, and the *Caryatids*, whenever Brancusi deals with the human subject, the object he creates represents only a part (or the parts, as in *A Muse* and *Mlle. Pogany*) of the larger organism, the natural image having submitted to a radical cutting off of elements. The resulting partial figure, to use Albert Elsen's term, is directly indebted to Rodin, and in adapting this invention to his own devices, Brancusi rationalizes it, as he rationalizes all: it gives him the cue to deal with the human figure in terms of limited *objects* which serve his ultimate purpose, that of essentializing form.

But Brancusi goes beyond the obvious cutting-off of the torso, of legs, of a hand in the case of *The Prayer*, and of the rest of the body in the case of *A Hand*. Throughout the sculpture there is an *omission* of anatomical parts that is not due to cutting, that is often unnoticed, always witty, and essentially magical. *Little French Girl* has no arms, but they are not cut off and there would be no place to put them; only late in the study of this work do we observe that they are missing. The genitals, in the case of *Torso of a Young Man*, have been omitted, and their absence causes no crisis of identity (*usually*, one must say, for Kenneth Clark has taken this to be a female figure). In *The Kiss* Brancusi solves the eternal problem—"What happens to the noses?"—by having them disappear. A number of heads have no neck. *The Chief* shows a mouth, the *White Negress* lips, but neither has eyes, nose or ears: while *Princess X, Eileen*, the *Nancy Cunard*, and the *Mrs. Meyer* have none of these features. *Narcissus Fountain* has one arm. *Bird in Space* has no wings or feathers; the *Fish*, no fins; *The Cock*, neither comb nor wattles; *The Turtle*, no hind legs.

When we consider the elimination of features which results from the rationalization of form, the cutting-off of parts, and the sheer absence of others, it is a kind of miracle that an image, and

a memorable one, remains. That it does is the sure sign of a
vision of the world that looked beyond appearances.

p.

With the exception of versions of *Mlle. Pogany* (and possibly of
A Muse), works characterized by constantly changing and unpre-
dictable views, Brancusi's sculpture, considered simply as form, is
apprehended immediately. The observer knows what is there at a
glance; further examination yields no surprises. Brancusi achieves
formal clarity by several means: a pervasive symmetry, a limited
number of axes, and rigorously articulated axes and surfaces. In
the spatial geometry of Brancusi we never drift or wander, but
always know where we are and how we got there.

q.

    We now see how necessary it was, just prior to 1915, to
abandon the representation of two or more objects touching each
other: the addition of a new element to a precariously balanced
gestalt would almost certainly create confusion. Given this
limitation, clarity is likely to be achieved in the simple mass or in
a longish design, and most of Brancusi's conceptions after this
point are in these formats. The long design is susceptible to
variation by a bending or curving of the axis, variety of profile,
and the serial accumulation of elements. Never again does
Brancusi place forms alongside each other as in *A Muse* and
the *Penguins*.
    From 1915 on, the Brancusian image is intelligible only in its
entirety. The date is that of *The Newborn*. In the earlier and
similar head, *The First Cry*, bold as the design may be, the nose
and mouth are represented. In the marble of *The Newborn* (p)
only the nose is represented; in the bronze (q) Brancusi dispenses
with even this representation. From this point on, except for the
lips of *White Negress*, 1923, and the mouth of *The Chief*, 1925,
he never again, in a new conception, delineates a specific feature
of a natural subject. In any case, the enterprise henceforth is one
in which he must create any image from invented elements and
relations, that is, from purely sculptural materials. Since henceforth there are no representational data, meaning is carried by all
that is there. Every work will be a gestalt to which every element
will contribute, and which will only be intelligible totally. This
may be tested by scanning or by a partial reading of the sculpture;
in works before *The Newborn* it is possible to grasp the image
when only a small portion of the sculpture is visible.

Limited as Brancusi's formal means seems to be, they are of a
variety equal to that of his representations and their changing
expressive needs. In themselves they constitute a subject of study.
    The sculpture explores the gamut of static states, but no work
of Brancusi's is positioned off its center of gravity and then
attached to a base.
    The most stable of the mature works is the massive, squarish
The Kiss, carved very early. Here the state of equilibrium is per-

fectly fitted to the subject, at the same time that the unproblematic treatment provides a base, as it were, for Brancusi's exploration of equilibrium. The stability of the first *Kiss* is repeated in its later versions; we see it in those other groups, *Double Caryatid* and the *Penguins*, and in *Wisdom of the Earth* and *Portrait of George*. When the stable mass rises to greater height than *The Kiss* of Montparnasse, it loses verisimilitude, the image becoming highly stylized as in the two versions of *Caryatid*. At even greater height it is only allusively figural, as in *King of Kings*. When it goes to great height, as does *Endless Column*, it becomes repetitive and decorative; no longer able to figure the human, it becomes a crystalline image. In the universe of Brancusi the mass of squarish section produces columnar objects; it is deployed horizontally only in the case of useful objects—wood and stone benches.

Starting with some children's heads, progressing through *Sleeping Muse*, *Prometheus*, *Sculpture for the Blind* and *Cup*, Brancusi makes a number of ovoidal, quasi-spherical and hemispherical sculptures. Their axes are generally lateral, they are in stable or neutral equilibrium, and they touch their bases on only a small area. When the axis of a round-bottomed sculpture is vertical the work is unstable and must be attached to a base; in the case of *Princess X* and *Torso of a Girl*, the sculptor has reserved a small plane on the work where it makes contact with its base.

Bird in Space is the climax of a series of precariously balanced vertical forms. *Fish*, Brancusi's thinnest sculpture and the one with the greatest lateral extension, is perfectly unstable; it must be attached to a base. *Nocturnal Animal* is transitional between *Fish* and *Turtle*, with something of the horizontality of the one and the flatness of the other. *Turtle*, relatively flat, parallel to the earth, and meant to be seen from above, is Brancusi's last original motif, and the last of a series—*Bird in Space*, *Fish*, *The Turtle*—that explores earthly space.

The Cock, with its forked axis, follows *Bird in Space*, and in the matter of equilibrium, is a variation of it; *The Seal* with its bent axis, is in the same relation to *Fish*.

Little French Girl, *The Sorceress*, *Chimera* and *Socrates* explore top-heavy forms on slender legs.

Up to 1921 Brancusian form may be said to exist around an axis; after that date, this axis moves to the surface and the rear, as a kind of spine, or, in the case of *Nocturnal Animal* and *Flying Turtle*, to the bottom. Until 1920 the sculpture is variously symmetrical and asymmetrical; after that date it is always essentially symmetrical.

The objects are not always fixed to bases. Some may be handled, other may rest in more than one position, and two may be set in motion. That aesthetic distance that we habitually associate with the work of Brancusi disappears, of course, in the case of objects meant to be handled.

The majority of works are clearly delimited objects, but those on disks are in *situations* not limited by their surfaces, and the same may be said of the large outdoor works in Tirgu Jiu.

The status of sculpture as object is put in question by a series of works created by *superimposition* of a number of objects: *Pasarea Maiastra, Chimera, Architectural Project, Exotic Plant, Adam and Eve, Boundary Marker.*

r.

While the majority of the sculptures are solid and monolithic, however venturesome of profile, *Prodigal Son* is much excavated, three works are pierced, and several are constructed.

The series *Endless Column, King of Kings,* and *Exotic Plant* explores repetition, variety, and close-valued changes.

Prodigal Son (r), radically asymmetrical, created by a great number of operations in an unfathomable order, and *Timidity* (s), created by two operations in an order that is certain, represent the extremes of sculptural economy in the oeuvre.

s.

Except for the monumental works, Brancusi's sculpture varies in size from *Sleeping Child*, hardly more than six inches long, to *King of Kings*, ten feet tall, with most of the works nearer the smaller figure; Brancusi had no wish to overwhelm the spectator by size, and claimed that the great contribution of Rodin to modern art was his return to a sculpture of human scale.

In spite of the preponderance of smooth and polished works in the oeuvre, many kinds of surface are to be found—variously textured modelling, rough and *non-finito* carving, gilded and patinated bronze—and often more than one are found in a single piece.

t.

But the reflective surface that Brancusi introduces in his polished bronze sculpture is his master device: it aerates the solid form, carries the drawing of the surface to an absolute state, and allows the accidental to play over his realm of certainty.

Brancusi has the curious faculty of continuing old themes while developing new ones, of recapitulating his past in terms that keep pace, as it were, with the evolving present. Thus the motif of *The Kiss* is pursued for a span of over thirty-five years, always recognizably *The Kiss*, always in stone, foursquare, and resting on a flat bottom, but undergoing changes of proportion, degree of stylization, and function. Twenty-seven related *Birds*, made in the course of thirty years, comprise a series that slowly changes in form and meaning and culminates in a version three times as tall as the first. *Mlle. Pogany*, in three marble versions and nine casts in bronze made between 1912 and 1933, maintains the same size while the motif is revised to a state just this side of abstraction.

u.

A long series that moved through many variations of form and significance while always keeping a relation to the theme of the human head begins with the quite explicit portrait, *Baroness R.F.* (t). This work soon leads to the more summary *Sleeping Muse* (u),

v.

w.

x.

y

z.

done from the same model. Only the memory of a human head remains in *Sculpture for the Blind*, and this form is refined to its limit in *Beginning of the World* (v), where the sleeping human head is seen as a metaphorical egg of creation. The conception can hardly be carried further, but the shape itself appears useful to Brancusi. To deal further with it he must complicate it. He lifts it from its naturally recumbent position, stands it on end to return it to the alertness and precariousness of developed humanity, and adds to it some signs of the human: lips, a neck, a crown, a chignon. These additions have such formal variety as to permit him to make several altogether different structures in a new series of heads in spite of the ovoid that is basic to all of them.

An important series—so small, so diverse in subject, so spread out in time as not to appear to be a series—is one comprised of *The Sorceress* (1916), *Torso of a Young Man*, the *Turtle* in wood, and the *Turtle* in marble (1945). If *Sleeping Muse* and its derivations explore the question of formal unity, these works are concerned with formal complexity. Indeed *The Sorceress* (w), because of the disposition of its masses and the relative multiplicity of its axes, is one of Brancusi's few obviously complex works. Soon after it is begun Brancusi makes *Torso of a Young Man* (x), an image that incorporates the two cylinders at a right angle to each that are evident in *The Sorceress*. The cylinders now rest on a base rather than being cantilevered; these are attached to a third member that is also a cylinder and that lies virtually on the same plane with them. Vertical, frontal, of only slightly disturbed symmetry, *Torso of a Young Man* is more compact and more immediately intelligible than *The Sorceress*.

The question of axial complexity (or of elements developing from a central mass) is taken up again in *Turtle* (y), also in wood. The sharp joinery of the *Torso* is absent here as legs and neck progress from the body in a more organic fashion; and the closeness and side-by-side repetition of the legs of the *Torso* have been dispersed in the *Turtle* by the interposed neck. But while it is reasonable that *three* elements radiate from a central *mass* (in contrast to *two* elements forking off a *length*, as in the *Torso*) the increase in the number of axes can hardly be considered an advance, that advance in economy that usually characterizes a new member of a Brancusian series.

This situation is resolved in the marble *Turtle* (z). A single form —roughly hemispherical, with a wedge removed—now includes both body and legs; the neck, a long tapering mass of squarish section, moves out between the legs from the high point of the body. Brancusi has been able to render three anatomical features of the wooden *Turtle* in a single mass, and the fourth in the only extension the work shows, avoiding the repetition of axes evident in the wood. All features diminish from the high point of the body to the perimeter of the work (in contrast to the wooden neck and legs whose extremities are larger than their point of origin), keeping them strong in the more frangible marble, but also increasing unity. The edge visible at the joining of neck and body is high—not a crease, as in the joinery to be seen in *Torso* and the wooden *Turtle*—and not disruptive. The relatively long neck is strong enough to support its length and blunt enough to resist accident in its exposed position. The *Flying Turtle* develops not only the immediate problems posed by the *Turtle* in wood; it seems to solve for Brancusi the long-standing problem of showing a relatively complex image in a relatively unitary form. For *Turtle* is Brancusi's last original design.

It has been evident for some time that the sculpture of Brancusi is strung out in thematic series, and that the themes are both formal and iconic. It is also evident that these series cross and recross, and that certain sculptures are then the nodes through which two or more themes pass. In this sense the image of the oeuvre is that of a network of interests.

The conviction develops that the oeuvre is shaped and controlled as carefully as any of its parts. It is almost as difficult to consider in isolation a single work as it is to consider a part of any sculpture. The sense of an artistic universe is enforced by the scope of subject and the gamut of formal concern. It is enhanced by another curious effect: just as there are no unsuccessful Brancusis or grave lapses in quality, so are there no towering peaks whose achievement sets them apart from the rest. The occasions of heightened or intense expressiveness seem to be balanced by a number of subdued works. The sense of a norm, of a pervasive evenness, is what one would expect of an effort to project a continuous field.

The creation of a unified oeuvre would be an achievement unique in the history of these matters. How, one wonders, would an artist go about planning it? There is no evidence to think that, in this sense, Brancusi began with a plan, nor is it easy to imagine how a life's work of the complexity of Brancusi's could be conceived in advance. But we may imagine the oeuvre slowly taking shape, at first without and then with the conscious direction of the sculptor. By 1913 he had created five works—*The Kiss, Narcissus, Sleeping Muse, Pasarea Maiastra* and *The First Step*—which are different from each other formally and poetically, and to which all other works of the period relate. The character of his imagination is such that the oeuvre after this period develops from these works by a number of means and so continuously that, with the exception of *Endless Column*, it is difficult to distinguish a subsequent theme that is unrelated to them.

Working quickly when he worked, he had time to dream his life and plan his art. He said to Ezra Pound, "*Toutes mes sculptures datent de quinze ans.*" ("All my sculptures start fifteen years back.") He conceived no new motif after *Flying Turtle*, 1945; he completed his last work in 1949. In 1952 he said to a visitor, "My work is finished." It is a work marvellously varied and marvellously continuous; it touches the real world and reaches toward the most difficult abstraction; it includes pure sculptural exercises and revelations of a personal nature; it reverberates beyond itself and is in constant reflection upon itself; it is an essay in the problems of sculpture and an exposition of the working of the creative imagination; and in spite of its scope, it is so shaped, and marked with such interplay of singularity and repetition, as to be able to be held in the mind. Brancusi's artistic uniqueness lies not so much in the invention of forms as in the making of relationships.

Because of his extraordinary concentration on his task, he was early caught in the meshing of every aspect of an existence in which morality influenced esthetic, and creation altered biography; where life and art, reacting upon each other at every moment, moved forward under the sign of inevitability. So he said to the sculptor Militza Patrascu, a student of his in the twenties, "You are lucky, you may do whatever you wish." His was a rare life whose intensity of purpose reacted upon it so that is was shaped by that purpose, in a dialectic that permitted no action to take place outside itself, and no effect to be unused or "left over." Brancusi's integrity of vision, issuing from a singular human nature with a special background and at a propitious moment in artistic history, seems fated.

Brancusi, as we noted earlier, looked beyond appearances. Then where did he look? It must be said, as he himself did, that his vision was attuned to a realm of essences and, eventually, the absolute. The simplicity that he achieved "in spite of" himself was a reduction to the essential—an effort that arose from no artistic principle or method, or from a striving for new form. He was critical of what he called *pompier* simplicity, that academic artistic simplicity which was a facile modern style.

The Brancusian simplicity was total, embracing the life and the work; it was the result of an unflagging search for the real. The real he found in the essential, in his existence no less than in his art. It is the unity of the life and the art that makes Brancusi an exemplary figure: a force both moral and artistic.

a. THE KISS. 1910. Montparnasse Cemetery

b. TORSO OF A YOUNG MAN. 1917. Cleveland Museum

c TORSO OF A YOUNG WOMAN. 1922. Philadelphia Museum

d. Rodin. THE KISS. 1886

e. THE KISS. 1912. Philadelphia Museum

f. Bourdelle. THE ARCHER. 1909. Metropolitan Museum, New York

g. Matisse. THE SLAVE. 1900–03. Baltimore Museum

h. Archipenko. BOXERS. 1914. Guggenheim Museum, New York

i. HEAD OF A GIRL (lost). 1907

j. BARONESS R. F. 1909

k. HEAD. 1908? Apollinaire Collection, Paris

l. HEAD OF A WOMAN. 1925. Levin Collection, Detroit

m. WHITE NEGRESS. 1923. Philadelphia Museum

n. EILEEN. 1923? Musée d'Art Moderne, Paris

o. THE CHIEF. 1925. Lambert Collection, Chicago

p. THE NEWBORN. 1915. Philadelphia Museum

q. THE NEWBORN. 1915. Museum of Modern Art, New York

r. PRODIGAL SON. 1915. Philadelphia Museum

s. TIMIDITY. 1917. Musée d'Art Moderne, Paris

t. BARONESS R. F. 1909

u. SLEEPING MUSE. 1910. Hirshhorn Collection

v. BEGINNING OF THE WORLD. 1920? James Clark Collection, Dallas

w. THE SORCERESS. 1916–22? Guggenheim Museum, New York

x. TORSO OF A YOUNG MAN. 1916. Philadelphia Museum

y. TURTLE. 1943. Musée d'Art Moderne, Paris

z. FLYING TURTLE. 1940–45? Guggenheim Museum

Note on the Catalogue

When more than one measurement is given, the order is: height, width, depth.

All foundry marks include the words *"cire perdue,"* omitted here.

The first notation under *"References"* is, in all but one case, the number of the work in a recent monograph by the author (Geist, 1968) whose virtual completeness makes it useful for easy reference (the data in this catalogue, where different from those in the monograph, supercede them) other notations refer to illustrations, since discussions of individual works are rare in the literature.

Our numbered references to the illustrations in *This Quarter*, 1925, not numbered in the magazine, are identified in Appendix I.

Works in the Exhibition

VITELIUS

Plaster, 24″ (61 cm.) high, 1898
Inscribed: C Brâncuș 1898
Collection Muzeul de Arta, Craiova

Provenance
Muzeul Stiintelor Naturale, Craiova

No exhibitions

References
Geist no. 2
Geist, Oct. 1964, p. 51

The work was discovered in Craiova in 1942; a bronze cast was made in Bucharest in 1964.

The earliest existing sculpture by Brancusi is a study from the antique, a portrait of the Roman emperor Vitellius, done at the Bucharest School of Fine Arts. Working from a plaster cast (recently found in Bucharest by B. Brezianu) Brancusi has made a version somehow more sympathetic than the original. He has replaced the turned base with a simple plinth which to modern eyes must count as an improvement; it is, at any rate, perfectly adjusted to his own study. He has also put a "z" on the title where there should be an "s", showing a carelessness of orthography which will be permanent. Brancusi, not yet 23, was awarded an honorable mention for this effort.

PRIDE

Bronze, 12 1/4″ (31 cm.) high, 1905
Inscribed: C BRANCUSI
Foundry mark: C. Valsuani
Collection Mr. and Mrs. Ralph F. Colin, New York;
   acquired 1955

Provenance
Curt Valentin Gallery, New York
Mrs. George Farquhar, New York
Mrs. Percival Farquhar, acquired from the artist

Exhibitions
Salon d'Automne, Paris, 1906, no. 220 (plaster)
Knoedler Gallery, New York, 1960

References
Geist no. 20b
Zervos, 1957, p. 21 (plaster)
Colin Collection, 1960, pl. 119
Sandulescu, 1965, pls. 1, 2

Dated by the inscription on another cast, in the Muzeul de
Arta, Craiova.

Pride was done at the Ecole des Beaux-Arts in Paris, thus
some time after June 23, 1905. It is modeled in a conventional and modest style, the symmetrical face and neck
enveloped by the irregular hair. Its very reserve seems to
command attention, which it repays: the head is beautifully
fashioned and firmly constructed; against its stability, we
read the counterpoint of the hair, with its different joinery
on the right and left sides.

   Pride is the first bronze cast by the artist. It is also his
first work with a symbolic title.

   Why *Pride*, when the expression shows none, when it is
if anything, neutral? A photograph of Brancusi's studio
shows an earlier state of *Pride* with a curious work placed
before it—a small sculpture of a young woman averting her
head from an unattractive man who attempts to kiss her.
The girl is the girl in *Pride*, the man resembles Brancusi—his
hair, like the sculptor's, falls in a bang over his brow. In the
title *Pride* Brancusi may be repaying the girl for a painful
rebuff.

Brancusi's studio, 10 Place de la Bourse, 1905

BUST OF A BOY

Bronze, 13 3/4″ (35.0 cm.) high, 1906
Inscribed: Brâncuși Paris 1906
Collection George Oprescu, Bucharest

Provenance
Victor N. Popp, acquired from the artist

Exhibitions
Salon d'Automne, Paris, 1906, no. 219 (plaster)
Muzeul de Arta, Bucharest, 1956–57, no. 5

References
Geist no. 22b
Oprea, 1960, p. 190
Jianou, 1963, pl. 105

Another cast is known to exist; a lost carving (Geist no. 45)
seems to be based on the work.

The easy facture and bold cutting-off of the right side show
the influence of Rodin, but the reserve is Brancusi's. After
his many straightforward, frontal portraits, this bust with
its inclined head and veiled glance is a new achievement
for Brancusi; it may be a portrait of a child who was blind.

SLEEPING CHILD

Bronze, 6 1/4″ (15.9 cm.) long, 1908
Inscribed: C. Brâncuși
Collection Mr. and Mrs. Malcolm C. Eisenberg, Philadelphia

Provenance
Mrs. Maurice Speiser, acquired 1921 by gift from the artist

Exhibitions
Brummer Gallery, New York, 1926, no. 1, illus. pl. 1
  Arts Club of Chicago, 1927
Philadelphia Museum, 1963

References
Geist no. 47a
M. M., 1923, p. 55 (plaster)
Giedion-Welcker, 1959, pl. 15 (plaster)
Geist, 1964, p. 69

Three other casts are known, two of which are inscribed "1908"; the treatment of the right side of the head varies.

We may suppose that this work, like so many others by Brancusi thought to be based on conventional themes, had a real model, who, however, has not been identified. The "1908" of the inscriptions is very likely the date of casting, the work probably having been modeled in 1906. This would accord with Rodin's praise of Brancusi's contributions to the Salon and his advice to the Rumanian not to work too fast. Indeed, in the last years of his life, Brancusi told his neighbor, Oscar Chelimsky, the American painter, that he had made three pieces in one afternoon.

Although the work was apparently executed with speed, it is a charming rendition of a sleeping child, and probably the sculptor's first essay of the subject of sleep and of the *head as object*.

In the original plaster (Musée d'Art Moderne, Paris) it is clear that a curl of hair just above the brow has been broken off, possibly during removal of the mold; the bronze records the plaster faithfully here. Brancusi has made no attempt to repair or tamper with the break, and evinces a curious acquiescence to fate which is not unique in his career. He imposes his design, but does not resist certain accidents, whether caused by him or resulting from other forces.

SLEEPING CHILD

Marble, 6 3/4″ (17.1 cm.) long, 1908?
Not inscribed
Collection Yolanda Penteado, São Paulo; acquired
  ca. 1950–52 from the artist

Exhibitions
Guggenheim Museum, New York, 1955–56
  Philadelphia Museum, 1956

References
Geist no. 50
Lewis, 1957, pl. 6
Zervos, 1957, p. 101

The work is dated by the supposed date of the plaster of
Sleeping Child (coll. Eisenberg), above. A slightly smaller
version, whose right side is not developed, is in the Musée
d'Art Moderne, Paris.

This head is a copy of the plaster of *Sleeping Child*, page x,
even to the missing curl of hair, which has not been
rendered as if there were no hair at that point, but as if it
had been *carved away*, thus repeating in the marble the
effect of the accident to the plaster. But Brancusi has not
copied the unfinished right cheek of the original; the marble is
fully developed on all sides; the end of the neck is slightly
concave. The hair, though rendered summarily with a point
for the most part, shows surfaces taken with the bush
hammer; and although the form of the face is firm and
smooth of surface, Brancusi has not erased the marks left
by rasping in certain areas. This tightly designed work
retains the evidence of its varied facture; but its naturalism
is somewhat at odds with its condition as an object.

TORMENT

Bronze, 14 1/4'' (36,2 cm.) high, 1907
Inscribed: C Brâncusi
Collection Mrs. Stanca Fotino-Morar, Bucharest

Provenance
Georges Fotino, Bucharest
Puis-Servien Coculescu
Nicolas Coculescu
Victor N. Popp, aquired from the artist

Exhibitions
Société Nationale, Paris, 1907, no. 1818 (plaster)
7th Tinerimea Artistica, Bucharest, no. 160, illus.

References
Geist no. 30.
Geist and Spear 1966, pl. 2

The work is dated by the exhibition of the plaster in the Salon de la Société Nationale, Paris, April 1907; Brezianu, 1964, p. 392. Another bronze is known.

Torment derives from a similar work done several months before, toward the end of 1906. That study (Geist no. 27) survives only in a photograph, but gives evidence of the often uninspired origin of many of Brancusi's definitive conceptions. In *Torment* the upright head has been moved against the shoulder in a gesture of pain, and every feature of the originally banal image has been raised to a state of significance. The head itself, possibly influenced by Medardo Rosso, is especially beautiful. With great tact Brancusi has suppressed all emotion on the face where the least grimace would have made contemplation of the work difficult. The real poignancy of *Torment* arises from the total image.

TORMENT II

Bronze, 11 1/2" (29.9 cm.) high, 1907
Inscribed: C BRANCUSI 1907
Foundry mark: C. Valsuani
Collection Richard S. Davis, New York; acquired ca. 1954

Provenance
Curt Valentin Gallery, New York, acquired by 1946

Exhibitions
Société Nationale, Paris, 1907, no. 1818 (plaster)
Cincinnati Art Museum, 1946, no. 1
Museum of Fine Arts, Houston, 1953, no. 11, illus.
Guggenheim Museum, New York, 1955–56
    Philadelphia Museum, 1956

References
Geist no. 31 a
Ritchie, 1952, p. 60

There is another cast of this work in Bucharest.

In making this version of *Torment*, Brancusi has decreased the height of the original by removing the lower portion that includes the roughly modeled left forearm and the ambiguous shape on which it rests. This manner of concentrating the image was already employed in the case of *Pride* and apparently in the case of a plaster *Head of a Boy* in the Muzeul de Arta R.S.R., Bucharest.

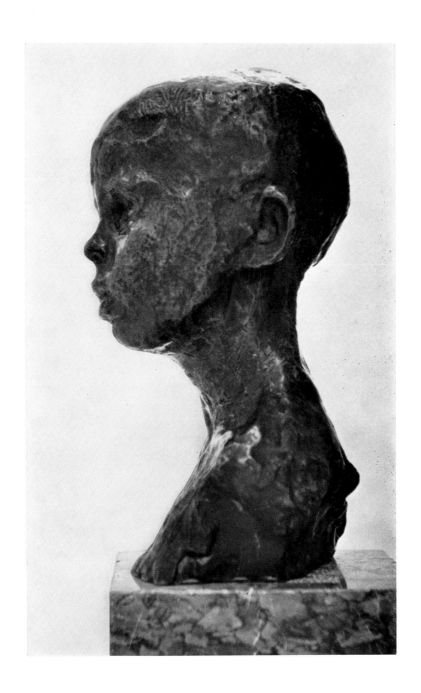

HEAD OF A BOY

Bronze, 13 1/2" (34.5 cm.) high, 1907
Inscribed: C BANCUŞI PARIS
Foundry mark: C. Valsuani
Collection Muzeul de Arta R. S. R., Bucharest; acquired
   1956

Exhibitions
Société Nationale, Paris, 1907, no. 1819 (plaster)
Muzeul de Arta, Bucharest, 1956–57, no. 2
Musée National d'Art Moderne, Paris 1961, no. 147
Künstlerhaus, Vienna, 1963, no. 125

References
Geist no. 32a
Jianou, 1963, pl. 7
Catalogue of Documenta, Kassel, 1964

A photograph of the plaster bears the message in Brancusi's
hand that this is the *Ebauche* shown at the Société
Nationale, Paris, April 1907; see Nicoara 1966. Two other
bronzes are known, one having the foundry mark of
A. A. Hébrard. This is the first work of Brancusi's to have
as many as three casts; all are in Rumanian collections.

In its modest scope this alert and noble head concentrates
all of Brancusi's abilities at this point and shows him to be
the master of anatomy, psychology and a vivid modeling
style. *Head of a Boy* is his third study, at least, of a child
done within a year.

THE PRAYER

Bronze, 43 7/8" (111.4 cm.) high, 1907
Inscribed: C BRACUȘI [and on the back] CRISTE CRSITE
Collection Muzeul de Arta R. S. R., Bucharest; acquired in
    1957

Provenance
Mrs. Eliza Popovici (ex Stanescu), commissioned from the
    artist

Exhibitions
26th Salon des Indépendants, Paris, 1910, no. 717
    (plaster? bronze?)
14th Tinerimea Artistica, Bucharest, 1914, no. 45
Muzeul de Arta, Bucharest, 1914, no. 45
Belgrade, 1959
    Budapest, 1959
    Bratislava, 1960
    Prague, 1960
    East Berlin, 1960
Musée Rodin, Paris, 1961, no. 224
Musée National d'Art Moderne Paris, 1961, no. 145
Künstlerhaus, Vienna, 1963, no. 126
Royal College of Art, London 1966, no. 5, illus. p. 9

References
Geist no. 36
Geist, Oct. 1964, pp. 48, 50
Giedion-Welcker, 1959, pl. 1 (plaster)
Jianou, 1963, pl. 11–13

In April 1907 Brancusi was commissioned to make a
monument for the grave of a lawyer in Buzau, Rumania.
A first payment made it possible for him to take a proper
studio on rue du Montparnasse (and leave the employ of
Rodin?); he soon executed a portrait and *The Prayer*.

Among Brancusi's effects (at the Musée d'Art Moderne)
is a photograph of a group of visitors in his studio;
reflected in the mirror behind them, one can see *The Prayer*,
in plaster. Among the visitors B. Brezianu, Bucharest, has
identified Nicolae Vaschide, a doctor and critic, of whose
wife Brancusi had done a portrait. Since Dr. Vaschide died
toward the end of 1907, what has been a matter of
speculation is now certain: that *The Prayer* was modeled
in 1907. The work was shown in Paris in 1910, though it
is not known in what material; the bronze was shown in
Bucharest in April 1914, and then installed, along with
Portrait of Petre Stanescu, in Dumbrava Cemetery,
Buzau.

As early sketch for *The Prayer* shows a woman so draped
as not to reveal her figure—a tactful conception for a grave.
It is, then, all the more noteworthy that Brancusi finally
made a fully revealed female figure, at a time when he was
dissatisfied with his recent figure studies; besides only the
male nude appears in the existing photographs of his
figure studies. We may suppose here the timely appearance
of a model toward whom the sculptor was attracted.

Because of his skill as a copyist, Brancusi's figure
studies may well have looked like the "cadavers" he
described them to be. In *The Prayer* he has made a great,
even violent, effort to create a figure with an independent
sculptural existence. He has compressed the natural
fleshiness and emphasized the changing directions of axes.
The arms and hands have been subjected, variously, to
removal, dislocation and extreme reduction. The right eye
is indicated by a pinch of material stuck to the flat eye
socket; there is no left eye. The whole figure is enveloped
in a surface of extraordinary variety, including deep pitting
at the back. Following a primitive impulse Brancusi has
incised two words on the back, starting at the end of the
right scapula and reading down: CRISTE CRSITE. (The
variation of the second term is typical; Brancusi has
misspelled his own name in singing this piece.)

The Prayer, in short, absorbs a number of assaults on the
representation of the human figure at the same time that
it conserves resemblance; it marks Brancusi's first move in
the direction of artistic independence. Now sixty-two years
old, it hardly shows its age; but its timelessness was hard
won.

The first of two studies (preserved in photographs in the
Brancusi Bequest, Musée d'Art Moderne) shows a kneeling
robed woman, crumpled in anguish, hands covering the
face, the long hair (or sackcloth?) flung forward and
falling almost to the knees; the whole is mounted on the
top of the tomb, to which several steps give access. The
conception is conventional, the mood hysterical, and the
modeling undistinguished. The second study, barely visible,
is, in its pose and leanness of form, close to the final work;
but an arm appears to be flung around the head in a
gesture of despair, while the whole figure leans over an
actual cavity that opens below it. The last grim detail is
mitigated in the final version where the figure simply
looks at the ground.

Thus, *The Prayer*, with its clarity, dignity and compression of sentiment, is not a mere sum of violences or
frustrations. Brancusi has not leaped to a solution, but
arrived at a final statement by the criticism, reworking and
distillation of a quite ordinary conception—a pattern which
will often be repeated in the years ahead.

THE KISS

Stone, 11″ (28.0 cm.) high, 1907
Inscribed: Brancusi
Collection Muzeul de Arta, Craiova

Provenance
Victor N. Popp, gift from the artist, 1910

Exhibitions
Armory Show, New York, 1913, no. 616 (plaster)
   Chicago, 1913, no. 24 (plaster)
   Boston, 1913, no. 6 (plaster)
"Contimporanul," Bucharest, 1924, no. 104
25th Tinerimea Artistica, Bucharest, 1928, no. 198 (plaster)
Week of Oltenia, Craiova, 1943, no. 14
City Art Museum of St. Louis, 1946, no. 80 (plaster)
Muzeul de Arta, Bucharest, 1956–57, no. 7 (plaster) and no. 8
Musée National d'Art Moderne, Paris, 1961, no. 143
Künstlerhaus, Vienna, 1963, no. 128
Royal College of Art, London, 1966, no. 7, illus. cover

References
Geist no. 39
Oprea, 1960, p. 194
Giedion-Welcker, 1959, pls. 37, 38
Jianou, 1963, pl. 15

Dated by statement in *This Quarter*, 1925, p. 264: "In 1907
he . . . began '*la taille directe*' with *le Baiser et la sagesse*."

The Kiss is related to Derain's earlier *Crouching Figure* by
size, material, carving method, massiveness of design, and
emphasis on hands and embracing arms. Derain's work
was shown at Daniel Kahnweiler's gallery on rue Vignon in
the fall of 1907, a short time before *The Kiss* was carved,
and it is likely that Brancusi saw it.

If *Pride* is part of an episode of a kiss refused, *The Kiss*
is a monument to a consummated kiss. There are good
reasons for seeing Brancusi in the male protagonist and a
friend of the artist in the female.

The Kiss, probably the second of Brancusi's direct
carvings in limestone, may be considered as the opening
movement of his career as a mature artist. Its gentleness
of expression, tender theme, and modest scale set a mode
from which he will rarely stray. The blending of the
personal and the universal, like the mixture of external
influence and independent invention, is typical of much
that will follow. Unique in the oeuvre are the absolute
stability and low center of gravity of this piece.

Of special interest is the fact that early and in a massive
work Brancusi achieves that immediate apprehension of the
motif which is such a striking feature of the later, and
leaner, works. What he will accomplish in these by means
of an extreme reductiveness or clarity of axis, is here
accomplished by the rationality of the design: any view
of the work supposes a situation on those facades which
are not in view. Yet the reading of the work proceeds slowly
as we register small notations symmetrically disposed,
which are at once sexual distinctions and formal
oppositions.

In spite of its probable debt to Derain, Brancusi's work
has a force of sentiment and a logic of design not evident
in *Crouching Figure*. The latter is a stylistic triumph, and as
such is inscribed in art history. *The Kiss* is a modern contribution to the mythology of love.

THE WISDOM OF THE EARTH

Stone, 19 7/8″ (50.5 cm.) high, 1907
Not inscribed
Collection Muzeul de Arta R. S. R., Bucharest

Provenance
Gheorghe Romascu, acquired 1910 from the artist

Exhibitions
9th Tinerimea Artistica, Bucharest, 1910, no. 245
Belgrade, 1959
    Budapest, 1959
XXX Biennale, Venice, 1960, no. 1
Musée National d'Art Moderne, Paris, 1961, no. 144
Royal College of Art, London 1966, no. 9, illus. p. 16

References
Geist no. 40
Geist, Oct. 1964, p. 51

Dated like *The Kiss*, above; but possibly early 1908. Though made in Paris, the work was first exhibited in Rumania where it remained. In both French and Rumanian (*Sagesse de la terre, Cumintenia pamintului*) the first word of the title refers to social or moral propriety in the sense in which it is used in French in the admonition: *Sois sage!*

Wisdom of the Earth has affinities with ancient cult figures and Egyptian sculpture. Except for the arms, the pose is very similar to that of the figures in *The Kiss* of Cimetière Montparnasse. From other knowledge of Brancusi's working habits we may suppose that this work, with its suggestive title, is not his first and only contact with the image; it may have been suggested by one or both of two lost earlier works (Geist nos. 33, 34) begun in 1907: round-faced heads of an Oriental cast.

   The meeting of arm, hand and breast is treated in a curiously flaccid fashion, and Brancusi will avoid such complications in the future. If, similarly, he will never repeat the captured space between the body and legs or the somewhat dangerously projecting shelf of the feet, these features are nevertheless adjusted to each other. In spite of the problems it presents, *Wisdom of the Earth* is one of Brancusi's most touching images, and one of the very few that are anatomically complete. Innocent, exposed, this personage shows a timeless calm and self-containment.

TORSO

Plaster, 9 5/8″ (24.4 cm.) high, 1909
Inscribed: C. Brancusi
Collection Mr. and Mrs. Harold Diamond, New York,
    acquired 1964

Provenance
Lucien Lefebvre-Foinet, Paris, acquired ca. 1936 from the
    artist

Exhibitions
8th Arta Romana Bucharest, no. 1 (plaster)
Muzeul de Arta, Bucharest, 1956, no. 9 (plaster)
Royal College of Art, London, 1966, no. 8 (plaster)

References
Geist and Spear, 1966, pl. 3

The work is dated in Brezianu, *Secolul XX*, 1967, and in
another version of this article, Brezianu, 1969, p. 27.

The marble original (Geist no. 51) is in the Muzeul de
Arta, Craiova; another cast is on view in the Brancusi
Studio, the Musée d'Art Moderne, Paris. A later and some-
what larger version in marble is in a private collection in
Stuttgart.

Barbu Brezianu, the Rumanian authority on Brancusi, has
recorded the following episode from the sojourn in Paris of
Clara Marbe, Ploesti, a friend of Marie Laurencin, Brancusi,
Modigliani and Kisling: in the summer of 1909, Miss Marbe
visited Brancusi in his studio at 54 rue du Montparnasse, in
the rear of the court, where he was working on *Torso* from
her friend, Lilly Waldenberg.

The image in *Torso* is that of a curiously limited portion
of a female figure, tenderly observed and fashioned. The
fragmentary nature of the work is not in itself remarkable,
since Brancusi has violated the wholeness of human anatomy
before this. What is curious here is that the work seems to
imitate a fragment broken from a larger work, rather than be
a designed fragment. Visible from one moment of vision is
the central part of the left side of a figure; beyond the profile
thus presented there is rough, uncarved stone. We may
wonder if Brancusi wished to make a fragment more radical
than any by Rodin.

But we note with surprise that what appears to be a
delicate invention, had a living model; and with further
surprise that it was *carved from life*—a not very common
practise. The smallness of *Torso* is in accord with the fact
that it had to be carved in a reasonable number of posing
sessions. The combination of realism and practicality is of
the essence Brancusian.

SLEEPING MUSE

Bronze, 11″ (28 cm.) long, 1910
Inscribed: BRNCUSI
Foundry mark: C. Valsuani
Collection Arthur Jerome Eddy Memorial, The Art Institute
  of Chicago; acquired 1931

Provenance
Arthur Jerome Eddy, acquired before 1914

Exhibitions
Albert Hall, London, 1913
Art Institute of Chicago, 1922, no. 8
University of Chicago, 1934, no. 4
Museum of Modern Art, New York, 1936, no. 16
  Cleveland Museum of Art, 1937
Cincinnati Art Museum, 1944, no. 3

References
Geist no. 57a
De Micheli, 1966, pl. I and cover illus.

Dated by the inscription on a similar bronze in the Musée National d'Art Moderne, Paris. In all there are five bronzes from the marble in the Joseph Hirshhorn Collection.

The number of bronzes, a second version in alabaster and its bronzes, the reappearance of the head in an altogether different work and its bronzes—all testify to the fascination the theme, and doubtless the model, held for Brancusi.

It should be noted that the bronzes from the first version of *Sleeping Muse* differ from each other in surface characteristics, and are variously shorter than the original by amounts not accounted for by shrinkage due to casting or by mere finishing of the bronze. These differences in length are evidence of considerable reworking, either on plaster or wax casts. None of these bronzes seem to have been polished to the reflective state of the bronzes of the second version (and, indeed, since their surfaces are far from absolute, a reflective polish would be disturbing); this may signify that they were all cast before *Maiastra*, 1911, a highly polished bronze.

In defiance of natural relationships, Brancusi has placed the ears so far to the rear that on that life-sized head they are only about two inches apart. This device, the closed eyes and recumbent position continue to make this work Brancusi's first fully successful *head as an object*, a magical evocation of sleep. Yet it is interesting to observe that the marble was originally carved with the eyes open; the lids were later effaced. Thus the work was probably intended to be vertical and alert in expression, and the model never assumed this pose for the artist.

SLEEPING MUSE

Bronze, 10 3/4″ (27.2 cm.) long, 1910
Inscribed: BRANCUS
Foundry mark: C. Valsuani
Collection The Metropolitan Museum of Art, New York,
    The Alfred Stieglitz Collection, 1949

Provenance
Alfred Stieglitz, acquired 1914 from the artist

Exhibitions
Gallery of the Photo-Secession, New York, 1914, no. 4
Philadelphia Museum, 1944, no. 109
Museum of Modern Art, New York, 1947, no. 1

References
Geist no. 57d

Dated by the inscription on a similar bronze in the Musée
National d'Art Moderne, Paris.

Sleeping Muse, *1909–10, coll. Joseph H. Hirshhorn,
New York*

45

PORTRAIT OF GEORGE

Marble, 9 3/8″ (23.8 cm.) high, 1911
Not inscribed
Collection The Solomon R. Guggenheim Museum,
  New York, 1956

Provenance
Mr. and Mrs. George Farquhar, New York
Mrs. Percival Farquhar, commissioned from the artist

Exhibitions
XXX Biennale, Venice, 1960, p. 33, no. 2
Arts Club of Chicago, 1960, no. 2

References
Geist no. 64
The Arts, 1957, cover illus.
Jianou, 1963, pl. 22

This work is a portrait of George Farquhar, born in Paris on November 10, 1910; his mother was Rumanian, his father American, a financier.

Portrait of George was done as a commission, which accounts for the fact that its realism seems out of place when seen in the context of Brancusi's other preoccupations in 1911. But it bears a strong resemblance to two children's heads that he had done some time before, and he may have considered it as a variation on them rather than as an interruption of the course of his invention. The head, indeed, is in a style somewhat different from that of the arm. The deep groove under the chin and along the arms is an unusual device; it causes a separation of elements—a constant feature in Brancusi's sculpture.

This tender work is the fullest and most explicit of Brancusi's many evocations of childhood and innocence.

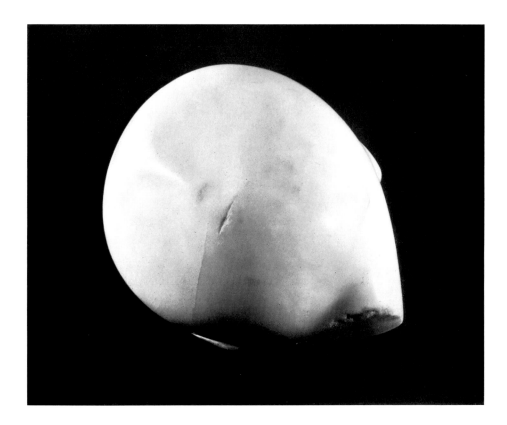

PROMETHEUS

Marble, 7″ (17.8 cm.) long, 1911
Inscribed: C. Brancusi
Collection Philadelphia Museum of Art,
   The Louise and Walter Arensberg Collection; by bequest,
   1950

Provenance
Walter Arensberg, acquired 1933 via Marcel Duchamp
John Quinn, acquired 1919 from the artist

Exhibitions
28th Salon des Indépendants, Paris, 1912, no. 495
Sculptor's Gallery, New York, 1922, no. 10
The Art Center, New York, 1926, no. 88
Brummer Gallery, New York, 1926, no. 6, pl. 6
   Arts Club of Chicago, 1927
Art Institute of Chicago, 1949, no. 6, illus.
Philadelphia Museum, 1954, no. 4, illus.
Guggenheim Museum, New York, 1955–56
   Philadelphia Museum, 1956

References
Geist no. 62
Zervos, 1957, p. 34
Lewis, 1957, pl. 8
Giedion-Welcker, 1959, pl. 13
Jianou, 1963, pl. 37

Dated by the listing in the 1926 Brummer catalogue; also
by the inscription—1911—on the bronzes.

Prometheus is a carving of a roundish head and a small
part of a neck, and is thus formally like the upper portion of
the lost *Narcissus*. The head is markedly broader than deep;
the features are in even more delicate relief than those of
Narcissus. Only the ears disturb the continuity of the mass;
unlike those of *Sleeping Muse*, they are far apart and
distributed asymmetrically with respect to the axis of the
head. If *Sleeping Muse* revealed a Brancusian tendency to
concentrated unitary form, *Prometheus* goes even further in
that direction.

   The head is inclined to one side in a gesture of pain that
Brancusi used in *Torment* and *The Redskins* and that
characterizes the head of *Laokoön*, the subject of his first
study at the Bucharest School of Fine Arts. In effect, then,
we have here a head of a child burdened with the Prome-
thean fate. The head was a portrait of an actual child, now a
man whom it still resembles; the title may reveal Brancusi's
feelings about the real difficulties surrounding the birth of
the child.

PROMETHEUS

Bronze, *7"* (17.8 cm.) long, 1911
Inscribed: C Brâncuşi
Joseph H. Hirshhorn Collection, New York

Provenance
Tarsila de Amaral, São Paulo, acquired 1926 from the artist

Exhibitions
Sociedade Pro-Arte Moderna, São Paulo, 1933
Galerie Europe, Paris, 1961, no. 1
Svensk-Franska Konstgalleriet, Stockholm, 1961, no. 28,
 illus.
Guggenheim Museum, New York, 1962–63, no. 40, illus.

References
Geist no. 63a

The two bronzes in the exhibition are the only ones which
have been recorded.

In the bronze of *Prometheus* Brancusi has effaced the faint
indications of eyes and the incised mouth of the marble.
The nuances possible in granular marble are sacrificed for
the sweeping effects of polished metal. While the marble
is a human image of extreme delicacy, the bronzes are
resplendent orbs with only a minimal human presence.

PROMETHEUS

Bronze, *7″* (17.8 cm.) long, 1911
Inscribed: C. Brâncuşi
Collection Mrs. Howard M. Kinney, Washington, D.C.;
    Gift from the artist

No exhibitions

References
Geist no. 63b

Maiastra *in the Steichen garden at Voulangis, on the outskirts of Paris, 1911*

MAIASTRA

Bronze, 21 3/4″ (55.3 cm.) high, 1911 ?
Not inscribed
Foundry mark: C. Valsuani
Collection Kate Rodina Steichen, New York

Provenance
Edward Steichen, acquired 1911 from the artist

Exhibitions
27th Salon des Indépendants, Paris, 1911, not listed
American Art Association, New York, 1923, no. 109
Guggenheim Museum, New York, 1955–56
    Philadelphia Museum, 1956
Knoedler Gallery, New York, 1966, no. 97, illus.

References
Geist no. 70a

Shown *hors catalogue* at the Salon des Indépendants, Paris, April 1911, according to Athena T. Spear in *The Burlington Magazine*, March 1969. Under the element that represents the legs, this example has a squarish plate that is not integral with the rest of the cast, but appears to be attached to it. Since this plate is a counterpart of a similar, slightly thicker one in an early state of the marble there is no doubt that this *Maiastra* is the first of four that Brancusi made, the other three lacking, like the marble in its present state, a plate under the legs. It was mounted on two stone bases and a tall post, together measuring about ten feet, in the garden of the Steichen house at Voulangis, and, in an old photograph, appears to have a highly polished surface. It would thus be the first of Brancusi's polished bronzes.

The base is apparently ancient. Brancusi owned it at a time when the recarved *Woman Looking Into a Mirror* was complete; he made at least two drawings from the motif which appears on it in relief.

   Like *The Kiss*, *Maiastra* results from a set of designs imposed from the front, the sides and the back. Here a curved system merges the views, while information is deployed hierarchically: most at the front, less on the sides, least at the back.

   This *Maiastra* is the shortest of the four bronzes; it seems a bit squat, perhaps because of the plate under the legs. In the bronze Brancusi has removed some material from the left side of the head, giving it the appearance of turning slightly to the right.

   Maiastra is a heraldic presence, noble and gentle.

MAIASTRA

Polished bronze, 24" (61.0 cm.) high, 1912
Inscribed: C BRANCUSI PARIS 1912
    [printed with punches]
Collection: John Cowles, Minneapolis

Provenance
Sidney Janis Gallery, New York
Theodore Schempp, Paris
N. N. Hovannessian, Paris

Exhibitions
"Contimporanul," Bucharest, 1924, no. 105
Exposition d'Art Roumain, Bucharest, 1927, no. 277, illus.
Tinerimea Artistica, Bucharest, 1928, no. 195
The Hague, 1930, no. 208, illus.
Galerie Giroux, Brussels, 1930, no. 214
Sidney Janis Gallery, New York, 1958, no. 6

References
Geist no. 71

Surely the third version in bronze of this theme, *Maiastra*
lacks the plate—a stylization of claws—present in the first
bronze, is greater in girth and more than two inches taller.
These increased dimensions, at the same time that the
size of the head remains constant, alter the proportions of
Maiastra and give it a new grandeur.

MAIASTRA

Polished bronze, 24 1/8″ (61.2 cm.) high
Collection Peggy Guggenheim Foundation, Venice;
   acquired 1940

Provenance
Paul Poiret, acquired ca. 1912 from the artist

Exhibitions
Art of This Century Gallery, New York, 1942, illus. p. 34
XXIV Biennale di Venezia, 1948, no. 12
Palais des Beaux-Arts, Brussels, 1951, no. 16
   Stedelijk Museum, Amsterdam, 1951, no. 16
Stedelijk Museum, Amsterdam, July 1951, illus. opp. p. 81
Tate Gallery, London, 1964–65, no. 43, illus. p. 37
Guggenheim Museum, New York, 1969, illus. p. 31

References
Geist no. 72
Guggenheim, 1942, p. 34
Lewis, 1957, pl. 50
Zervos, 1957, p. 37
Giedion-Welcker, 1959, pl. 58
Guggenheim, 1960, p. 73
Jianou, 1963, pls. 43–44
Calas, N. and E., 1966, no. 60

Dated by the Cowles *Maiastra*, inscribed 1912.

The *Maiastra* theme finds its culmination in this bronze, the
fullest and tallest of all five versions. It is most like the
previous *Maiastra* in its proportions and grandeur, but the
gently rounded edges of the latter are here sharp and
definitive.

THE KISS

Stone, 23″ (58.4 cm.) high, 1912
Inscribed: Brancusi
Collection Philadelphia Museum of Art,
    The Louise and Walter Arensberg Collection; by bequest,
    1950

Provenance
Walter Arensberg, acquired 1932 via Marcel Duchamp
John Quinn, acquired 1916 from the artist

Exhibitions
28th Salon des Indépendants, Paris, 1912, no. 496
Sculptor's Gallery, New York, 1922, no. 6
Brummer Gallery, New York, 1926, no. 4, pl. 4
    Arts Club of Chicago, 1927
Museum of Modern Art, Moscow, 1928, no. 6
Art Institute of Chicago, 1949, no. 5, illus.
Philadelphia Museum, 1954, no. 3, illus.
Guggenheim Museum, New York, 1955–56
    Philadelphia Museum, 1956
Munson-Williams-Proctor Institute, Utica, New York, 1963,
    no. 616, illus.
    69th Regiment Armory, New York, 1963
Museum of Fine Arts, Houston, 1965
Expo 67, Montreal, 1967, no. 72, illus.

References
Geist no. 65
Foster, 1922, p. 68
Ritchie, 1952, p. 106
Zervos, 1957, p. 25
Adrian, 1956–57, p. 239
Lewis, 1957, pl. 12
Giedion-Welcker, 1959, pl. 39
Dictionnaire de la Sculpture Moderne, 1960, p. 34
Jianou, 1963, p. 92
Selz, 1963, fig. 211

The work is dated 1912 in the Sculptor's Gallery catalogue,
1922. It was probably exhibited as no. 496 at the Salon des
Indépendants, Paris, March 20–May 16, 1912.

This third version of *The Kiss* carries further the stylization
of the first version already evident in *The Kiss* of the
Cimetière Montparnasse. More block-like than the latter, all
of its elements lie even closer to the large planes of the
work: the hands and arms are very shallow and the heads
are quite four-square. Lacking the sensitivity of touch and
changes of depth of the first version and the richness of
design of the second, it has become an almost impersonal
didactic rendering of an idea in an only slightly relieved
mass. But it has its own incisiveness due to a new emphasis
on the paired eyes and the woman's breasts and chest,
turned with a care not evident in any other version of this
work.

   In a letter of October 4, 1916, to Walter Pach, Brancusi
says of this work, "With regard to a base for the Kiss it will
be preferable to put it just as it is on something separate for
any sort of arrangement will look like an amputation."

A MUSE

Marble, 17 1/2" (44.5 cm.) high, 1912
Inscribed: C BRANCUSI
Collection The Solomon R. Guggenheim Museum, New York,
    Gift of Ardé Bulova, 1958

Provenance
Ardé Bulova, acquired at auction, 1955
Mr. and Mrs. Charles J. Liebman
A. B. Davies, acquired 1914 from the artist, via Alfred Stieglitz

Exhibitions
Armory Show, New York, 1913, no. 618 (plaster)
    Art Institute of Chicago, 1913, no. 26 (plaster)
    Copley Society of Boston, 1913, no. 8 (plaster)
Gallery of the Photo-Secession, New York, 1914, no. 8
Sculptor's Gallery, New York, 1922, no. 25
Columbus Gallery of Fine Arts, Ohio, 1937, illus. (plaster)
Amherst College, Amherst, Massachusetts, 1958 (plaster)
Arts Club of Chicago, 1960, no. 3
Munson-Williams-Proctor Institute, Utica, New York, 1963,
    no. 618, illus. p. 41
69th Regiment Armory, New York, 1963

References
Geist no. 66
M. M., 1923, p. 24
Jianou, 1963, pl. 27
Spear, 1966, pl. 6

A plaster cast of this work (coll. The Solomon R. Guggenheim Museum) was exhibited in the Armory Show, February
1913; its exhibition tag (in the Walt Kuhn Papers, The
Archives of American Art, New York) bears the date 1912.
The work was listed as "8. NAIADE-MARBLE" in Brancusi's
exhibition at the Gallery of the Photo-Secession in 1914.

A Muse, like *Portrait of George*, is achieved by the addition
of new elements to a motif already at hand. But it is Brancusi's peculiar feat in *A Muse*, a wakeful image, to have
incorporated almost unaltered an image of sleep, *Sleeping
Muse*. The eyes here have been effaced almost completely;
the right cheek rather than the left is now the fuller of the
two. The bulging throat, for which there is no counterpart in
nature, is a daring invention in itself and contributes to the
sinuous movement which animates this frontal organization.

*"But the implacable Venus gazes far into the distance at
some object or other with her marble eyes"* (Charles
Baudelaire).

Pencil drawing of A Muse, *6 9/16" × 4 13/16", in a letter,
June 20, 1917, from Brancusi to John Quinn*

Margit Pogany, from a photograph taken in 1910

MLLE. POGANY

Marble, 17 1/2″ (44.5 cm.) high, 1912
Inscribed: C BRANCUSI
Collection Philadelphia Museum of Art,
    Gift of Mrs. Rodolphe M. de Schauensee, 1933

Provenance
Earl Horter
John Quinn, acquired 1914 from the artist, via Alfred Stieglitz

Exhibitions
Armory Show, New York, 1913, no. 619 (plaster)
    Art Institute of Chicago, 1913, no. 27 (plaster exhibited,
    marble illus.)
    Copley Society of Boston, 1913, no. 9 (plaster exhibited,
    marble illus.)
Mánes Society, Prague, 1914 (plaster)
Gallery of the Photo-Secession, New York, 1914, no. 2
The Art Center, New York, 1926, no. 87
Philadelphia Museum, 1928
Philadelphia Museum, 1940, no. 46
Philadelphia Museum, 1956

References
Geist no. 67
Eddy, 1914, p. 202
Rindge, 1929, pl. XXXVIII 4
American Magazine of Art, September 1933, p. 431
America and Alfred Stieglitz, 1934 pl. XIIc
Zervos, 1957, p. 43
Giedion-Welcker, 1959, pl. 24
Jianou, 1963, pl. 29
Hamilton, 1967, pl. 175

Dated, like *A Muse*, by the exhibition tag for the plaster
exhibited at the Armory Show, February 1913; the marble
was reproduced in the Chicago and Boston catalogues of
the same exhibition. The marble was probably first shown in
London in 1913; it was shown in 1914 at the Gallery of the
Photo-Secession in New York, where John Quinn bought it.
It caused a critical scandal in the Armory Show, turning an
unexpected attention on its creator; in the years since then
its fame has become such that it seems to be the archetype
of the human image in modern art. Arp called it "the fairy
godmother of abstract sculpture."[1]

The inspiration for *Mlle. Pogany* was Margit Pogany, a
Hungarian painter studying in Paris. By her account Brancusi,
who had observed her in a *pension* where they used to
have lunch in the summer of 1910, invited her to his studio
where he was much pleased that she recognized herself
—"all eyes"—in a little head he had made (*Narcissus?
Danaide?*). She asked Brancusi to do her portrait and he
was "greatly pleased" by her proposal. Her record of the
posing sessions is worth quoting: "I sat for him several
times. Each time he began and finished a new bust (in
clay). Each of these was beautiful and a wonderful likeness,
and each time I begged him to keep it and use it for the
definite bust—but he only laughed and threw it back into
the boxful of clay that stood in the corner of the studio—to
my great disappointment. Once I had to sit for my hands
but the pose was quite different to that of the present bust,
he only wanted to learn them by heart as he already knew
my head by heart." These sessions took place in December
1910 and January 1911. When Mlle. Pogany left Paris in
January the bust was not yet begun.

Mlle. Pogany continues the theme of the bust with arms that we see in *Woman Looking into a Mirror* (lost), *Portrait of George*, and *A Muse*. Whereas the latter work is organized frontally, *Mlle. Pogany* has a spiralling composition unique in the oeuvre. It is the least rationalized of all Brancusi's works, presenting a great number of aspects which are always surprising, and whose discovery demands more time than is usually the case in Brancusi's sculpture.

It hardly needs comparison with the model to see how bold Brancusi has been in making this portrait. He achieves a likeness which we recognize as more than epidermal and at the same time creates a head that has the largest eyes, the smallest mouth and the finest nose that one could imagine.

[1] Zervos, 1957, p. 30.

THREE PENGUINS

Marble, 22 1/2″ × 21 1/2″ × 13 3/4″
  (57.2 × 54.6 × 35.9 cm.), 1912?
Not inscribed
Collection Philadelphia Museum of Art,
  The Louise and Walter Arensberg Collection; by bequest,
  1950

Provenance
Walter Arensberg, acquired 1934 via Marcel Duchamp
John Quinn, acquired 1916
The Modern Gallery, New York

Exhibitions
The Modern Gallery, New York, 1916
Sculptor's Gallery, New York, 1922, no. 8
Brummer Gallery, New York, 1926, no. 8, pl. 8
  Arts Club of Chicago, 1927
Art Institute of Chicago, 1949, no. 8, illus.
Philadelphia Museum, 1954, no. 6, illus.
Guggenheim Museum, New York, 1955–56
  Philadelphia Museum, 1956

References
Geist no. 80
Pound, 1921, pl. 15
Zervos, 1934, p. 83
Gindertael, 1956, p. 14
Zervos, 1957, p. 51
Lewis, 1957, pl. 14
Giedion-Welcker, 1959, pl. 41
Jianou, 1963, pl. 34

A photograph of the sculpture in the Brancusi Bequest at the Musée d'Art Moderne, Paris, bears the date 1912 in the artist's hand. A listing in the 1926 Brummer catalogue reads: "8. Penguins 1914."

Aside from the several versions of *The Kiss* and the curious *Double Caryatid*, the *Penguins* are the only other group sculptures Brancusi made. Why should he have done penguins at all? It is true they had not been known for long, but Brancusi does not really explore their uniqueness; besides, their uniqueness or oddity would not seem to have recommended them to Brancusi's attention. What we see in the sculpture is a group of generalized birds which he calls "penguins."

We may well believe that Brancusi, in the early years of his stay in Paris, had socialist sympathies. His small study, *The Redskins*, was a tribute to the exploited natives of the American continent. One of his sculptures, possibly *Head of a Boy* (Geist no. 32), was exhibited in Bucharest in 1907 with the title, *Son of the Fields*. And that summer he contributed a work to an exhibition at the phalanstery of the Abbaye de Créteil. We note at this point that Anatole France, in the autumn of 1907, gave the Abbaye a manuscript of his to publish in order to help save it. Otilia de Cosmutza, a critic and journalist, was the mutual friend of these men. Brancusi had for over a year lived only a few doors from her on Ile St. Louis; it was in her home that he first met Baroness Frachon (the model for *Sleeping Muse*), according to the latter; and Mme. de Cosmutza had written laudatory reports of Brancusi's work for a Rumanian journal. She was a friend of Rodin and member of an international literary circle, but there is no doubt that Anatole France was the central figure in her life in this period. She knew him possibly for two years before accompanying him on a trip through France and Italy in 1910; in 1927 she published *Promenades avec Anatole France*. Brancusi was surely aware of France's *Penguin Island*, published in 1908, as he was of its author who, in the years that followed, became an ever more prominent public figure and defender of socialist causes.

There is, in a sense, iconographic support for *Penguin Island* as a literary source of *Three Penguins*. The novel is a satire on French history, and the penguins represent people. In Brancusi's sculpture we see only heads: these are partial figures—the only such in Brancusi's animal sculpture—but the usual mode in which he makes his human images.

Three Penguins was probably carved in 1912. Anatole France must have been much on Brancusi's mind when in July 1911 France, in a public letter, defended three jailed labor leaders who had gone on a hunger strike. It is just possible that we have here the source of the triple representation of penguins.

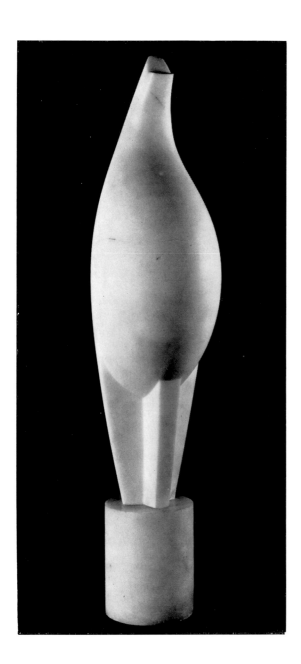

BIRD

Marble, 23 3/4″ (60.4 cm.) high, 1912?
Not inscribed
Collection Philadelphia Museum of Art,
    The Louise and Walter Arensberg Collection; by bequest,
    1950

Provenance
Walter Arensberg, acquired 1931 via Marcel Duchamp

Exhibitions
Art Institute of Chicago, 1949, no. 7
Philadelphia Museum, 1954, no. 5, illus.
Guggenheim Museum, New York, 1955–56
    Philadelphia Museum, 1956

References
Geist no. 69
Zervos, 1957, p. 35
Lewis, 1957, p. 51
Giedion-Welcker, 1959, p. 200, no. 2
Jianou, 1963, pl. 42

Bird cannot be dated with certainty, but there is no doubt
that it was carved between *Pasarea Maiastra*, 1910–12, and
Bird p. 69 dated 1915. It is one of four carvings of birds of
which Brancusi made no bronze versions; eight carved
birds have versions in bronze.

Brancusi's second carving of a bird shows a change in the
significance of the image and a corresponding change in its
formal character. No longer standing and speaking with neck
thrust forward, *Bird* calls to the heavens, its head pointing
upward, and the whole body showing now a gentle elongation. The body is less bulbous, the transition between it and
the tail is less abrupt, the neck does not show a sudden
change in section from that of the body, and the eyes have
disappeared. The elongation of the sculpture is echoed in
the base, not a squat block now, but a cylinder taller than it
is wide.

MLLE. POGANY

Polished bronze, with black patina, hair, 17 1/4"
  (43.8 cm.) high, 1913
Inscribed: Brancusi
Foundry mark: C. Valsuani
Collection The J. B. Speed Museum, Louisville,
  bequest of Mabel Hussey Degen, 1954

Provenance
Mabel Hussey Degen, acquired 1920's from the artist

Exhibitions
Dallas Museum of Fine Arts, 1965, no. 12, illus. p. 7

References
Geist no. 74c
The J. B. Speed Museum Bulletin, May 1955, cover illus.

In the autumn of 1913 Brancusi offered Margit Pogany a
bronze of *Mlle. Pogany* which he had apparently just
finished; it is assumed that the four recorded bronzes of this
work were cast in that year. These casts differ essentially
only in patina, not in their dimensions; the signatures vary,
and one copy has no foundry mark. The base of the Speed
version is not by the sculptor.

Brancusi cautioned Mlle. Pogany about touching the shiny
parts of the work with bare hands. To bring the marble to
this reflective metal state Brancusi has not merely polished
the cast—he has completely reworked the surface to a point
of absolute definition.

HEAD OF THE FIRST STEP

Wood, 10 1/4″ (25.9 cm.) high, 1913
Inscribed: C. Brâncuși
Collection Musée National d'Art Moderne, Paris; acquired
  1957 by bequest from the artist

Exhibitions
Gallery of the Photo-Secession, New York, 1914, no. 7
  (full figure)
Brummer Gallery, New York, 1926, no. 7, pl. 7;
  Arts Club of Chicago, 1927

References
Geist no. 76
Pound, 1921, pl. 16 (full figure)
America & Alfred Stieglitz, 1934, pl. XIIc (full figure)

Exhibited in March 1914 at the Gallery of the Photo-
Secession, New York, as part of *The First Step*, mistakenly
titled *The Prodigal Son* in the exhibition. When *Head of
First Step* was exhibited at the Brummer Gallery, 1926, it
was titled *Child's Head* and dated 1913.

The Farquhar family (see *Portrait of George*) believe the
pose of *The First Step* is based on a photograph they had,
and have misplaced, of Brancusi supporting the standing
infant George. Among Brancusi's effects, at the Musée
d'Art Moderne, Paris, there is a photograph of Brancusi
supporting a standing child.

Nothing in Brancusi's previous sculpture prepares us for
the developments in his earliest extant woodcarving. In
spite of the boldness of invention and unusual sensibility
which it manifests, the sculpture of Brancusi up to this
point is basically a version of European naturalism. As such
it does not exhibit the special primitivism of *The First Step*
and the striking treatment of the head in particular. *The
First Step* clearly supposes a knowledge of African Negro
sculpture; it has striking affinities with a woodcarving from
the Upper Niger region which was in the Musée d'Ethnologie
in 1916, and surely earlier. The groove cut along the nose is
anticipated by the more radical—and somewhat disruptive—
cutting on the later heads of *Jeannette*, 1911–12, by
Matisse. But neither this feature nor the hollowed-out
mouth disrupts the wholeness of Brancusi's work. The
economy of its massiveness is relieved by the raised edge
of the upper lip.

*Wooden figure, Upper
Niger, coll. Musée de
l'Homme, Paris*

The first Step, 1913,
wood, ca. 44″, destroyed

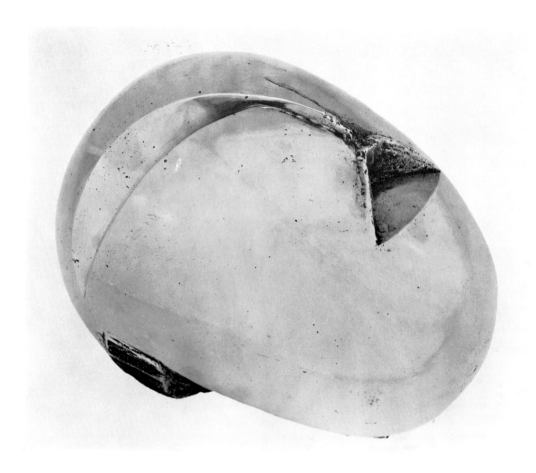

THE FIRST CRY

Polished bronze, 9 7/8″ (25.1 cm.) long, 1914
Inscribed: C. Brâncusi
Collection Isidore Cohen, New York, acquired 1968

Provenance
H. P. Roché

Exhibitions
Musée National d'Art Moderne, Paris, 1953, no. 110
Hotel de Ville, Yverdon, Switzerland, 1954, no. 26
   Kunsthaus, Zurich, 1954, no. 34
Guggenheim Museum, New York, 1955–56
   Philadelphia Museum, 1956
Museum des 20. Jahrhunderts, Vienna, 1964, no. 4, illus.

References
Geist no. 77a

Since a wooden figure including this head was exhibited
early in 1914, it is here supposed that the bronze casts were
made after the exhibition, and before *The Newborn*, 1915,
which derives from it. There are three bronzes with various
finishes.

The First Cry is the second case of a head, originally
oriented in an upright position, which was eventually placed
in a recumbent attitude; the first was *Sleeping Muse*. This
change in position will give rise to a whole series of similar
works.

LITTLE FRENCH GIRL

Oak, 49″ (124.5 cm.) high, 1914–1918?
Inscribed: C. Brâncuși
Collection The Solomon R. Guggenheim Museum,
    New York, Gift Katherine S. Dreier Estate, 1953

Provenance
Katherine S. Dreier, acquired early January 1920 from the
    artist

Exhibitions
Société Anonyme, New York, 1920
Brummer Gallery, New York, 1933–34, no. 55
Yale University Art Gallery, New Haven, 1952–53, no. 6,
    illus.
Guggenheim Museum, New York, 1955–56
    Philadelphia Museum, 1956
Arts Club of Chicago, 1960, no. 5

References
Geist no. 113
Pound, 1921, pl. 21 (unfinished)
Hamilton, 1953, p. 37
Jianou, 1963, pl. 67

The date for the beginning of the work is estimated on
purely stylistic grounds: its large design is related to that of
The First Step, 1913, whose nose and eye it copies, and
whose two legs it retains; its mouth mediates between those
of *The First Step* and *The Newborn*, 1915; the decoration on
the side of the head would seem to precede the similar
elements on *Caryatid*, 1915, in the Fogg Art Museum; and
its two legs would seem to precede the single legs of
Madame L. R., 1916, and *Socrates*, 1923. Its legs were
divided into three sections much after the work was begun,
possibly after this feature appeared on *Madame L. R.*

   It is very likely that *Little French Girl* was shown in
New York by The Société Anonyme in 1920; Marcel
Duchamp thought so.

Little French Girl, even more clearly than *The First Step*,
shows an African influence, especially that of Sudanese
sculpture. The repeated channeling caused by the gouge is
one of the few decorative notes in the oeuvre. This is the
first of Brancusi's constructed works; construction makes
possible the daring oppositions of form and size. Yet in
spite of these it is more unified stylistically than *The First
Step*, an incisive image, both touching and funny.

TWO PENGUINS

Marble, 21 1/4″ × 11 1/8″ × 12 1/8″
  (54.0 × 28.3 × 30.8 cm.), 1914
Inscribed: CB
Collection The Art Institute of Chicago,
  Ada Turnball Hertle Fund; acquired 1962 through Fine
  Arts Associates, New York

Provenance
Mrs. Ileana Bulova
Gladys Lloyd Robinson
H. P. Roché, acquired from the artist

Exhibitions
Gallery Guggenheim Jeune, London, 1938, no. 8
Musée National d'Art Moderne, Paris, 1953, no. 158
Guggenheim Museum, New York, 1955–56
  Philadelphia Museum, 1956
Fine Arts Associates, New York, 1956, no. 5
Dallas Museum for Contemporary Arts, 1959
Staempfli Gallery, New York, 1960, no. 4, illus.

References
Geist no. 81
Jianou, 1963, pl. 36

Dated by H. P. Roché in 1955, while the artist was still alive.

The earlier version has a disturbing captured space on its main facade, and the illusion of three separate bodies, the latter effect created by the rounded edges at the meeting of the large planes. In *Two Penguins* plane meets plane in abrupt fashion, making for greater actual continuity of the material. At the same time, largely by eliminating the smallest of the three birds, Brancusi has created a real spaciousness and a more easy articulation of large masses in *Two Penguins*. (If it was possible to theorize about the number of birds in *Three Penguins*, such theorizing is no longer possible here: the number of birds has been reduced for purely formal reasons.) As a result of these changes, *Two Penguins* is a rigorous, classic and witty image.

BIRD

Blue-gray marble, 27 3/4″ (70.5 cm.) high, 1915
Not inscribed
Collection Musée National d'Art Moderne, Paris; acquired
 1957 by bequest from the artist

No exhibitions

References
Geist no. 83
Giedion-Welcker, 1959, pls. 59, 68
Liberman, 1960, pl. 83

Dated in Giedion-Welcker, 1959, p. 124, probably from a
photograph dated by Brancusi. The work was broken early
and repaired by the artist.

Bird carries further the general elongation of this theme
already begun in the white marble *Bird* of the Arensberg
Collection. With the narrowing of all elements at the bottom
of the work, Brancusi has re-introduced a stylization of the
claws, apparently to make the legs intelligible as such. In
keeping with the smallness of the footing and the strong
sense of upward movement, he has made a base of reduced
massiveness which itself suggests movement. There is no
version in bronze; the sculptor possibly considered the
work to be transitional.

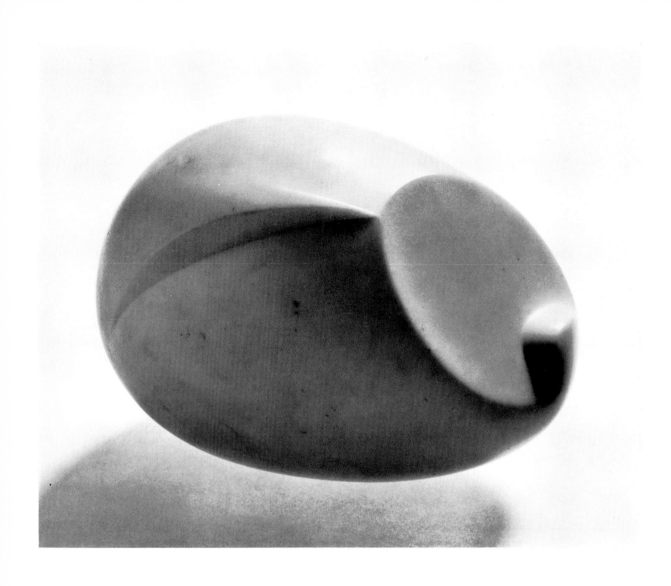

THE NEWBORN

Marble, 8 1/8" (20.7 cm.) long, 1915
Not inscribed
Collection Philadelphia Museum of Art,
    The Louise and Walter Arensberg Collection; by bequest,
    1950

Provenance
Walter Arensberg, acquired 1933 via Marcel Duchamp
John Quinn, acquired 1922
The Modern Gallery, New York

Exhibitions
Sculptor's Gallery, New York, 1922, no. 23
Brummer Gallery, New York, 1926, no. 5, pl. 5
    Arts Club of Chicago, 1927
Art Institute of Chicago, 1949, no. 11, illus.
Philadelphia Museum, 1954, no. 9, illus.
Guggenheim Museum, New York, 1955–56
    Philadelphia Museum, 1956

References
Geist no. 84
M. M., 1923, p. 20
Dreyfus, 1927, p. 72
Zervos, 1938, p. 323
Zervos, 1957, p. 49
Lewis, 1957, pl. 9
Giedion-Welcker, 1959, pl. 15
Jianou, 1963, pl. 35
Hamilton, 1967, pl. 176

The work is dated by the listing in the 1926 Brummer
catalogue. Two casts in bronze are known; there is another,
somewhat larger version in marble, and a bronze and a
stainless steel version from it.

The Newborn carries further the theme of *The First Cry*, a
crying child portrayed in a head without a neck, the head as
object. The marble simplifies radically the work in wood,
reducing the number of elements and planes; the eye and
mouth, sunken into the mass of *The First Cry*, are realized
here by the subtler means of a shift of the surface. But the
relieved nose, evident in the wood, is retained in the marble.
The Newborn is less imitative of nature even than *The First
Cry*, and creates a human image by relating a very few
abstract elements. This bawling head, meant to be handled
like so many of Brancusi's sculptures of children, presents
the pathos of birth with a compassionate humor.

The Newborn, *bronze, 1915, coll. The Museum of Modern
    Art, New York*

CARYATID II

Wood, 90 1/8″ (228.9 cm.) high, 1915
Not inscribed
Collection Musée National d'Art Moderne, Paris,
  Brancusi Bequest, 1957

Exhibitions
Guggenheim Museum, New York, 1955–56
  Philadelphia Museum, 1956

References
Geist no. 89
Giedion-Welcker, 1959, pl. 98

This work was dated by H. P. Roché at the time of the
Brancusi retrospective at The Solomon R. Guggenheim
Museum in 1955–56, while the sculptor was still alive.
There is no record of its previous exhibition. There is indeed
no early photograph of it, even by Brancusi, or any report of
its having been seen at an early date. It is remarkable that so
large an object should have escaped photography or other
attention for forty years.

Caryatid II would seem to have been carved after the *Caryatid* in the Fogg Art Museum, its size and large feet freeing
it from the base-like element of the smaller version. The
organic-looking torso has been countered by angular and
more structural elements, the whole work displaying similar
oppositions of massiveness and openness, unaccented area
and intense detail. *Caryatid II* has an unabashed innoncence
of stance and presence, and a primitivism that is African.

Caryatid, *wood, 1915, recarved in 1926, coll. Fogg Art
Museum, Cambridge, Massachusetts*

PRODIGAL SON

Oak, 17 1/2″ (44.5 cm) high, 1915
Not inscribed
Collection Philadelphia Museum of Art,
    The Louise and Walter Arensberg Collection; by bequest,
    1950

Provenance
Walter Arensberg, acquired ca. 1921

Exhibitions
Sculptor's Gallery, New York, 1922, no. 21
Brummer Gallery, New York, 1926, no. 22, pl. 22
    Arts Club of Chicago, 1927
Brummer Gallery, New York, 1933–34, no. 57
Art Institute of Chicago, 1949, no. 9
Philadelphia Museum, 1952, no. 8
Philadelphia Museum, 1954, no. 7, illus.
Guggenheim Museum, New York, 1955–56
    Philadelphia Museum, 1956

References
Geist no. 91
Pound, 1921, pl. 20
Einstein, 1931, pl. 622
Ritchie, 1952, p. 107
Zervos, 1957, p. 56
Giedion-Welcker, 1959, pls. 74, 75
Jianou, 1963, pl. 64
De Micheli, 1966, pl. VI

The dating of this work has caused confusion in the
Brancusi literature because a work in Brancusi's exhibition at
the Gallery of the Photo-Secession in 1914 was given the
title—by Stieglitz?—of *Prodigal Son*, and because of a typo-
graphical error in the Brummer catalogue of 1926, where an
illustration of it is dated 1925. It is correctly dated 1915
elsewhere in the Brummer catalogue. The work was not in
the Photo-Secession show; it is dated 1915 in *This Quarter*,
published in 1925.

Prodigal Son is easily Brancusi's most intricate and excavated work, the product of an unusual (for Brancusi)
number of operations on the material. Yet its open structure
is such as to be immediately intelligible, like Brancusi's
more solid unitary works. With its post, arch, fine engraving,
cantilevered mass, and play of curve and flatness, it shows
Brancusi as the master of a variety and asymmetry not
evidenced up to this moment.

    The image is difficult to decipher; it may show a kneeling
figure, one hand on the ground, a pack on its back. Albert
Elsen has suggested that the title refers to Brancusi himself;
and in fact Brancusi had made a trip to Rumania in 1914,
his first such trip since 1909.

SCULPTURE FOR THE BLIND

Marble, 11 3/8" (28.9 cm.) long, 1916?
Not inscribed
Collection Philadelphia Museum of Art,
    The Louise and Walter Arensberg Collection; by bequest,
    1950

Provenance
Walter Arensberg, acquired 1935 via Marcel Duchamp
John Quinn, acquired 1922 from the artist

Exhibitions
Brummer Gallery, New York, 1926, no. 32, pl. 32
    Arts Club of Chicago, 1927
Art Institute of Chicago, 1949, no. 20, illus.
Philadelphia Museum, 1954, no. 18, illus.
Guggenheim Museum, New York, 1955–56
    Philadelphia Museum, 1956

References
Geist no. 98
Valentiner, 1946, pl. 13
Lewis, 1957, p. 11
Giedion-Welcker, 1959, p. 66
Jianou, 1963, pl. 38
Burnham, 1968, p. 85

The work is dated by a text left by H. P. Roché: "This work
[*Beginning of the World*] came after 'the sculpture for the
blind' . . . which was (I think) exhibited at the Independents
in New York around 1917." That exhibition took place from
April 10 to May 6; the catalogue lists only *Princess X* by
Brancusi. But Roché's further description of the unusual
manner in which the work was exhibited, makes it very
probable that the work was shown somewhere in New
York and at that time to which he refers.

Sculpture for the Blind is gently faceted. It strikes one as a
muffled version of *Sleeping Muse*; both works have the
same length. Roché quotes the sculptor: "I put my curiosity
of the unknowable into it—an egg where little cubes seethe,
a human skull." *Sculpture for the Blind* is the latest of a
series of works that were meant to be touched; Brancusi
intended it to be a "revelation for the hands." It was
exhibited, Roché recalled, enclosed in a bag that had two
sleeves through which the hands could enter.

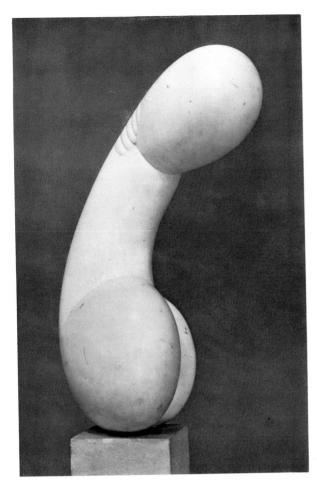

Since the work was acquired early in 1917 by John Quinn, and since a bronze of it was shown in New York in April 1917, it is reasonable to date it 1916; and it is so dated in the Brummer catalogue of 1926. But it was begun much earlier.

"I had heard that he had done a statue of a princess. I had seen one that he did about fourteen years before in marble of a very beautiful woman with her head slightly leaning on one side and nude to the waist. He had worked and worked on it until it was almost completely abstract and resembled the same object that Gaudier Brzeska's head of Ezra Pound did."[1] This remarkable text by the British artist, Nina Hamnett (1890–1956) is the only record of the fate of a work conventionally called *Woman Looking Into a Mirror* (of which only some photographs survive) and of its transformation into *Princess X*. Writing about an episode in 1920, Miss Hamnett's estimate of "fourteen years before" would place the beginning of the work in 1906, which is clearly improbable if we compare it with works whose 1906 date is certain. More reasonable for stylistic reasons is the date 1909. This was a year in which Brancusi traveled, was ill, did not produce much, and complained of his progress.

The early work was probably too diffuse for Brancusi; surely the textured hair—on the head, in a chignon on the neck, and cascading over the back and bosom—presents a problem both in its amount and its insistent contrast with the smooth areas. In any event, Brancusi eventually reduced the mass of the work by more than a half, eliminating its whole left side. The clarity of the final state is presaged by *Narcissus*, 1910? lost; the bold elimination of facial features was accomplished in *Narcissus Fountain*, 1914; the fully modeled breast is clearly related to the same feature in *Eve*, now known to have been carved in 1916.

In transforming the naturalistic image and raising the pitch of its sentiment to an extraordinary point, Brancusi retains the arching head and neck, the hand beside the breast, and the self-engrossment of the original. The great arc formed by the head and neck forces the material almost to a structural limit, creating a motif which is the very shape of narcissism. Quite innocently (as I think) Brancusi has created a shape that has proved inescapably phallic. This circumstance led eventually to the removal of the work from the Salon des Indépendants of 1920. Angered, Brancusi withdrew *Chimera* from an exhibition of "Section d'Or," and did not show again in Paris until 1926.

Princess X is the most precariously balanced and confectionary work in the Brancusi oeuvre. Other knowledge of Brancusi leads us to suppose an actual young woman as inspiration for the work in 1909. By 1916 the work had a new inspiration, an actual Rumanian princess, whose identity the sculptor preferred not to divulge.

[1] From *Laughing Torso* by Nina Hamnett. Long and Smith, New York, 1932, p. 123–24.

PRINCESS X

Marble, 23 1/8" (58.7 cm.) high, 1916
Not inscribed
Collection University of Nebraska Art Galleries,
  Gift of Mrs. A. B. Sheldon, 1963

Provenance
H. P. Roché
John Quinn, acquired March 1917 from Modern Gallery,
  New York

Exhibitions
Sculptor's Gallery, New York, 1922, no. 11
Brummer Gallery, New York, 1926, no. 15, pl. 15
  Arts Club of Chicago, 1927
Guggenheim Museum, New York, 1955–56
  Philadelphia Museum, 1956
XXX Biennale, Venice, 1960, no. 4, illus.

References
Geist no. 96
Zervos, 1957, pp. 52, 53
Giedion-Welcker, 1959, pl. 45

PRINCESS X

Polished bronze, 23″ (58.4 cm.) high, 1916
Not inscribed
Collection Philadelphia Museum of Art,
    The Louise and Walter Arensberg Collection; by bequest,
    1950

Provenance
Walter Arensberg, acquired ca. 1917

Exhibitions
Society of Independent Artists, New York, 1917, no. 167,
    illus.
Brummer Gallery, New York, 1926, no. 25, pl. 25
    Arts Club of Chicago, 1927
Art Institute of Chicago, 1949, no. 13, illus.
Philadelphia Museum, 1954, no. 11, illus.
Guggenheim Museum, New York, 1955–56
    Philadelphia Museum, 1956
II Documenta, Kassel, 1959, no. 2, illus. p. 21

References
Geist no. 97a
M. M., 1923, p. 28
Zervos, 1957, p. 55
Lewis, 1957, pl. 17
Giedion-Welcker, 1959, pl. 47
Jianou, 1963, pl. 33

This work was shown in New York, from April 10 to May 6,
1917, at the Society of Independent Artists; a photograph
in the catalogue shows it polished to mirror brightness. Two
other casts are known.

The bronze of *Princess X* does not exhibit the precious-
ness and attenuation of the material which threaten the
marble. The arc seems to express the more elastic quality of
the metal; every surface has been brought to an absolute
point in order to achieve unruffled reflectivity.

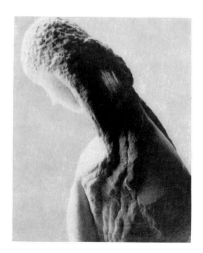

Woman Looking into a Mirror, *marble, 1909, recarved*

THE SORCERESS

Wood, 39 3/8″ (100 cm.) high, 1916–1922?
Inscribed: C Brancusi Paris 1916
Collection The Solomon R. Guggenheim Museum, New York;
acquired 1956 from the artist

Exhibitions

New Chenil Galleries, London, 1925, no. 2
Wildenstein Galleries, New York, 1926
Museum of Modern Art, Moscow, 1928, no. 5
Brummer Gallery, New York, 1933–34, no. 30
Palais des Beaux-Arts, Brussels, 1934, no. 15
Dum Umeni, Brno, Czechoslovakia, 1947
Guggenheim Museum, New York, 1955–56
  Philadelphia Museum, 1956
Arts Club of Chicago, 1960, no. 4, illus.

References

Geist no. 99
Zorach, *The Arts*, March 1926, p. 150
Einstein, 1931, pl. 623
Zervos, 1957, p. 57
Lewis, 1957, pl. 28
Giedion-Welcker, 1959, pls. 78–80
Jianou, 1963, pl. 65

Schematic drawing of Eve, *wood, in 1916, the dotted lines showing parts by 1919; see page 104*

The date inscribed on this work can only signify the year when it was begun, since it was certainly not completed until 1922 or even 1923: it appears, unfinished, in a photograph with the completed *Torso of a Girl*, 1922.

On the one hand, *The Sorceress* is related to *The First Step* (destroyed), *Madame L. R., Chimera, Little French Girl* and *Socrates*—top-heavy works which stand on one or two legs. But it is related, too, to *Torso of a Young Man* (made soon after it and also showing two cylinders) and *The Turtle*, the design of all three depending on a portion of a tree cut to include a crotch. Much as these relations demonstrate again the formal density of the Brancusian oeuvre, they do not help us to decipher *The Sorceress*. At this level we have only Brancusi's title and what appears to be a head wearing a cowl. Here I wish to propose a possible reading of this work.

The primary meaning of the French title, *La Sorcière*, is "the witch," and this is how Clive Bell referred to the work in an article published in 1926. In view of what remains of Brancusi's library, and of his interest in the occult, it is likely that he knew the classic *La Sorcière*, Jules Michelet's famous interpretation of the European witch-craze. Chapter 5, which deals with possession by the devil and with a distension of the body which this produces has the following passage: "Ce gonflement est un trait cruel de la *possession*; c'est un supplice et un orgueil. Elle porte son ventre en avant, l'orgueilleuse de Strasbourg, renverse sa tête en arrière." [1] (This swelling is a cruel mark of possession by the devil; it is a torment and a [cause for] pride. She walks with her belly thrust forward, the proud woman of [the Cathedral of] Strasbourg, she throws her head back.)

Could the last phrase have been read by one whose French was imperfect, "she turns her head to the rear"? If it is read this way we have a description of Brancusi's sculpture: the slanting leg figuring the stance of a woman with a swollen stomach, the head turned to the rear, the breasts facing the opposite direction. And it is now justifiable to see the two cylinders as breasts: in a photograph recently found among Brancusi's effects we see *Eve* in its original state, on a long vertical leg, standing beside the roughed-out *Sorceress*. The cylinders of the latter are in the same relative position as the more realistic breasts on the *Eve*, and look like geometrical versions of them.

In the sentence before the one we have examined, we note the words "torment" and "pride," the titles of two earlier works of Brancusi's. Twelve lines later we find "baroness," the title of another earlier work. If Brancusi, who thought of his life as fated, read this passage, he may have felt he "had to" make a *sorcière*.

[1] *La Sorcière* by Jules Michelet, Paris, Editions Julliard, p. 80.

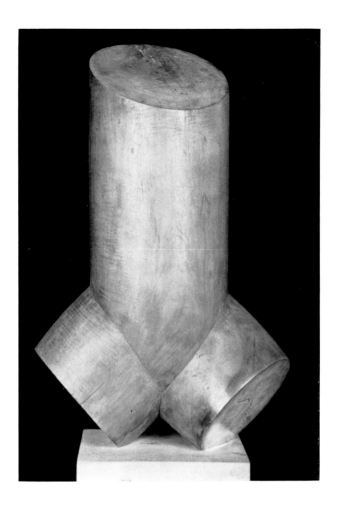

TORSO OF A YOUNG MAN

Maple, 19″ (48.3 cm.) high, 1916?
Inscribed: CB [in a circle, three times]
Collection Philadelphia Museum of Art,
    The Louise and Walter Arensberg Collection; by bequest,
    1950

Provenance
Walter Arensberg, acquired 1948
Stendahl Galleries, Hollywood
Josef von Sternberg, acquired late 1920's
John Quinn, acquired 1923

Exhibitions
Brummer Gallery, New York, 1926, no. 11, pl. 11
    Arts Club of Chicago, 1927
Art Institute of Chicago, 1949, no. 17, illus. p. 40
Philadelphia Museum, 1954, no. 15, illus.
Guggenheim Museum, New York, 1955–56
    Philadelphia Museum, 1956

References
Geist no. 100
M. M., 1923, p. 25
Zervos, 1957, p. 68
Lewis, 1957, pl. 21
Giedion-Welcker, 1959, pl. 35
Jianou, 1963, pl. 56
Licht, 1967, fig. 189

The work is dated by the bronze in the Cleveland Museum of Art, inscribed 1917.

Torso of a Young Man is related to the torso of the destroyed *First Step*, 1913, and more immediately to *The Sorceress*, 1916; like the latter it shows two cylinders at a right angle to each other and is carved in a piece of forked material.

The work is a fusion of the most diverse elements. Its fragmentary nature is surely indebted to Rodin, and it is Brancusi's contribution to have made of the fragment an independent object in which there is no sense of the cutting-off of parts. On the other hand, its wholly modern clarity is unthinkable without the influence of African art, already evident in *The First Step*.

The phallicism of the total image is rendered in a ratio-nalized mode exactly that of the breasts (as they now seem to be) of *The Sorceress*.

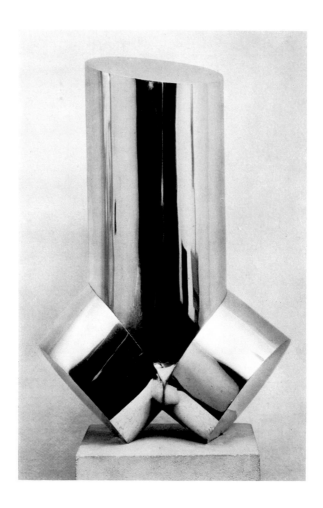

TORSO OF A YOUNG MAN

Polished bronze, 18 3/8″ (46.7 cm.) high, 1917
Inscribed: C Brancusi PARIS 1917
Collection The Cleveland Museum of Art, acquired with
    funds from Hinman B. Hurlbut Trust, 1937

Provenance
Brummer Gallery, New York, from the artist

Exhibitions
Brummer Gallery, New York, 1933–34, no. 14
Albright Art Gallery, Buffalo, New York, 1936, no. 125
Museum of Modern Art, New York, 1936, no. 20
    Cleveland Museum of Art, 1937
Museum of Art, Rhode Island School of Design, Providence,
    1950
Contemporary Arts Museum, Houston, 1958, illus. p. 22
William Rockhill Nelson Gallery of Art, Kansas City,
    Missouri, 1960, no. 115, illus. p. 35
Cleveland Museum of Art, 1960, no. 2, illus. pl. 2
Cleveland Museum of Art, 1966, no. 5

References
Geist no. 101 a

There is another bronze (Joseph H. Hirshhorn Collection)
inscribed 1922: this was the basis for the dating of *Torso of
a Young Man* until the recent discovery of the inscription on
the Cleveland bronze.

The version in metal is shorter than the wood by an amount
that accounts for the flatter slope of the upper plane. The
high polish, the absoluteness of design and the apparent
fusion of the geometrical and the human give this work a
quintessential modernity that must have been the more
dazzling when it was created, more than a half century ago.

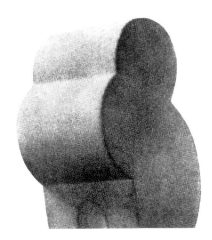

TIMIDITY

Stone, 14 3/8″ × 9 7/8″ × 8 5/8″
  (36.5 × 25.0 × 21.8 cm.), 1917
Inscribed: F 12 III B   C. Brancusi PARIS 1917
Collection Musée National d'Art Moderne, Paris; acquired
  1957 by bequest from the artist

Exhibitions
Brummer Gallery, New York, 1933–34, no. 12

References
Geist no. 88
Pound, 1921, pl. 22
This Quarter, 1925, pls. 15, 23
Zervos, 1957, p. 50
Giedion-Welcker, 1959, pls. 66, 68, 97
Liberman, 1960, pl. 83

The inscriptions "12" and "B" refer to the listing of the
work in the 1933–34 Brummer catalogue.

Timidity is unusual in the oeuvre in that it may be conceived
as having been made in two operations: the cutting of a
profile in a thick slab of material, and the carving of a
concavity on the rectangular plane produced. The distance
of the plane behind the mass overhanging it precludes the
possibility of the reverse order in these operations. The very
small number of operations, their known order, the rationality
of the design and its total massivity declare the work to be
diametrically opposed, in its formal character, to *Prodigal Son*.
    The scooped out feature appeared earlier in *Madame L. R.*;
this, in turn, seems to have been suggested by the space
created at the meeting of legs and torso in both versions of
Caryatid. *Timidity* is a most reserved female torso, the just
discernible human image rescuing it from mere design, even
as its seemingly mechanical mode of execution is relieved
by the one carved area.
    It has been remarked that its profile resembles that of many
of Modigliani's studies for a caryatid. One of these, in the
Norton Gallery and School of Art, West Palm Beach, has the
word, AUDACITÉ, printed across the top. We may speculate
that Brancusi's title, and the work itself, are commentaries
on his friend's drawing. But *Timidity* is not merely a work of
great reserve, but an example of sculptural ellipsis.

Madame L. R., *wood, 1914–17, coll. Mme. Nadia Léger,
  Biot, France*

CHIMERA

Oak, three sections, 59 3/4″ (152.3 cm.) high, 1918
Inscribed: Brancusi
Collection Philadelphia Museum of Art,
   The Louise and Walter Arensberg Collection; by bequest,
   1950

Provenance
Walter Arensberg, acquired 1938 via Marcel Duchamp
John Quinn, acquired June 1922
The Modern Gallery, New York

Exhibitions
Sculptor's Gallery, New York, 1922, no. 22
Brummer Gallery, New York, 1926, no. 9, pl. 9
   Arts Club of Chicago, 1927
New Burlington Galleries, London, 1936, no. 34
Gallery Guggenheim Jeune, London, 1938, no. 9
Art Institute of Chicago, 1949, no. 14, illus.
Philadelphia Museum, 1954, no. 14, illus.
Guggenheim Museum, New York, 1955–56
   Philadelphia Museum, 1956
Cleveland Museum of Art, 1966, no. 8

References
Geist no. 106
Pound, 1921, pl. 12
Zervos, 1957, p. 61
Lewis, 1957, pl. 24
Giedion-Welcker, 1959, pls. 76, 77
Jianou, 1963, pl. 62

This work is dated by the listing in the 1926 Brummer catalogue.

Chimera, as its title warns us, is one of Brancusi's disturbing images. It is difficult to decipher, seeming, like the duck-rabbit illusion, to alternate between two appearances: a girl's head at one moment, and, at another, a bird's head not unlike one of Brancusi's penguins.

   Formally it is a member of a series of works with top-heavy forms on slender legs. In *Chimera* this off-center form is not balanced on its leg, but held up by the strength of the material. The work is symmetrical from one view and asymmetrical from the view at a right angle to it, and may be conceived to result from the removal of part of one leg from a design originally symmetrical from both views.

Dated by a letter to John Quinn postmarked December 27, 1917, in which Brancusi wrote: "I have just finished the bronze and it leaves at the same time as this letter." He went on to say: "it turned out well and I have taken all precautions that it arrive in good condition and I hope you will be satisfied."

John Quinn first asked Brancusi for a bronze of *A Muse* in a letter written in mid-March 1917. On June 20 Brancusi wrote: "I have delayed a while in replying to you because I wanted to see if I could make a bronze that really would be a bronze and not simply a cast of the marble (a cast which would in my opinion be better in plaster) and for that I had to work a great deal." He was now in a position, he continued, to make the bronze, which would be completely finished by himself.

In a group of statements and aphorisms published in *This Quarter* in 1925 Brancusi said: "High polish is a necessity which relatively absolute forms demand of certain materials." It was to bring *A Muse*—with its stony shapes and roughly carved and unfinished areas—to the state of "absolute forms" that Brancusi had to "work a great deal." Aside from making many small changes he tipped the work forward and made it noticeably taller by adding to the bottom. In a second version in bronze, slightly shorter than the first, Brancusi carries the rationalization of all elements even further.

A Muse in bronze, lacking the faint indication of eyes and the personal quality of facture still visible in the marble, is of a modernity that separates it from any stone age, and announces the gleaming beauty of a new age of metal.

A MUSE

Polished bronze, 19 3/4" (50.2 cm.) high, 1917
Not inscribed
Collection Museum of Fine Arts, Houston; acquired 1962

Provenance
Earl Horter
John Quinn, acquired 1918 from the artist

Exhibitions
Sculptor's Gallery, New York, 1922, no. 19
Austin, Texas, 1968

References
Geist no. 102
Jianou, 1963, pl. 26

A MUSE

Polished bronze, 19 1/2″ (49.5 cm.) high, 1918
Inscribed: C. Brâncusi
Collection Portland Art Museum, Portland, Oregon,
    Gift of Miss Sally Lewis, 1959

Provenance
Sally Lewis, Portland, Oregon, acquired 1924

Exhibitions
American Art Association, New York, 1923 (as per statement
    of Sally Lewis; see Portland Art Association Annual Report,
    1959)
Guggenheim Museum, New York, 1955–56
    Philadelphia Museum, 1956
Portland Art Museum, 1963

References
Geist no. 103
Pound, 1921, pl. 12
M. M., 1923, p. 28
Zervos, 1957, p. 54
Lewis, 1957, pl. 18
Portland Art Association Annual Report, 1959, p. 2

SLEEPING MUSE II

Alabaster, 11 3/8″ (28.9 cm.) long, 1917
Inscribed: C. Brâncuşi
Collection Mrs. H. Gates Lloyd, Haverford, Pennsylvania;
    acquired 1944

Provenance
Peter Moon, Chicago
John Quinn, acquired 1919 from the artist

Exhibitions
Sculptor's Gallery, New York, 1922, no. 10
The Art Center, New York, 1926, no. 88
University of Chicago, 1934, no. 5
Staempfli Gallery, New York, 1960, no. 1
The Washington Gallery of Modern Art, Washington, D.C.,
    1963, no. 8

References
Geist no. 78
M. M., 1923, p. 15
Spear, 1966, pl. 3

Dated by a letter from Brancusi to John Quinn, postmarked Paris, December 27, 1917. The letter included a photograph of the work of which Brancusi said that it was "not yet finished but one can see the end."

Brancusi's letter, in refering to both *Yellow Bird* (Yale University Art Gallery) and this *Sleeping Muse* says: "They must not be considered as reproductions of the first ones, for they are conceived differently and I have not taken them up again simply to do them in another way, but to go further."

    Sleeping Muse II eliminates the short neck visible in the first version; instead a small finger of form protrudes below the chignon at the back. The ears are now closer together, a ridge separating them. But the changes on the face are more subdued (and this time they have been carved as though closed), and the eyebrows sweep upward in an form has been rendered, if anything, more fluid (aided by the translucency of the material), the bulge of the eyes is more subdued (and this time they have been carved as though closed), and the eyebrows sweep upward in an extraordinary fashion that defies nature. *Sleeping Muse II* is a more independent object than the first, a dream in stone.

SLEEPING MUSE II

Polished bronze, 10 3/4″ (27.3 cm.) long, 1926
Not inscribed
Collection Joseph Pulitzer, Jr., St. Louis, Missouri;
    acquired 1959

Provenance
Fine Arts Associates, New York, acquired 1959
Jean Cassou

Exhibitions
Hôtel de Ville, Yverdon, Switzerland, 1954, no. 25
Kunsthaus, Zurich, 1954, no. 33
Fine Arts Associates, New York, 1959, no. 4
City Art Museum, St. Louis, 1961, illus.
Fogg Art Museum, Cambridge, Massachusetts, 1961
City Art Museum, St. Louis, 1968, no. 86

References
Geist no. 79 e

Dated by its first owner. There are two other examples.

Sleeping Muse II was surely created with a polished metal version in view. At any rate the bronzes from this work are dazzling objects, evocations of sleep and feminine beauty whose blending of the fragilely human and the uncompromisingly metallic, supplies a new *frisson*.

ENDLESS COLUMN

Oak, 80″ × 10″ × 9 5/8″ (203.2 × 25.4 × 24.5 cm.), 1918
Inscribed: CB [in a circle]
Collection Mary Sisler, Palm Beach, Florida

Provenance
Jon N. Streep
H. P. Roché
John Quinn, acquired 1922 from the artist

Exhibitions
Brummer Gallery, New York, 1926, no. 31, pl. 31
  Arts Club of Chicago, 1927
Guggenheim Museum, New York, 1955–56
  Philadelphia Museum, 1956
Fine Arts Associates, New York, 1956, no. 6
Staempfli Gallery, New York, 1960, no. 6, illus.

References
Geist no. 108
Pound, 1921, pls. 7, 12
M. M., 1923, pp. 18, 22
Lewis, 1957, pl. 31
Jianou, 1963, pl. 70

Endless Column, *wood, in the Steichen garden at Voulangis,*
  ca. 1920

Dated in the 1926 Brummer catalogue.

If the lesser width of the rhomboids that compose *Endless Column* is given the value of 1, then the greater width has the value 2, and the height of each rhomboid has the value 4. We may imagine that the simplicity of this ratio, 1 : 2 : 4, and the fact that any deviation from it has a detrimental effect on the design, led Brancusi to say that he considered *Endless Column* to be one of his two works—the other being *The Cock*—in which he achieved something like ultimate perfection. [1]

Besides doing a study in plaster for a monumental column and designing the *Endless Column* of Tirgu Jiu, Brancusi carved four other columns, one of which was for some time in the garden of Edward Steichen's house at Voulangis. All the columns have half rhomboids at the top and bottom. Of the columns that had a public existence, the one in the exhibition has three full rhomboids, the Steichen *Column* had nine, and the *Column* at Tirgu Jiu has fifteen; we note, for what it may be worth, that all these numbers are odd and divisible by three. Yet when Brancusi showed portions of three columns at the Brummer Gallery in 1933–34, he cut them so that they would just fit into the twelve-foot-high room.

It seems that at first the Sisler *Column* was not intended to be an independent sculpture. When John Quinn inquired about a base for it, Roché replied that Brancusi had said it would not need a base "till it is put forever in a special place, supporting a special thing."

Endless Column, indeed, is not a sculpture in the sense that other works by Brancusi are. It is rather a decorative work, and one which, significantly, supplies Brancusi with the motif of many of his pedestals; the motif first appeared as the base of the marble *Bird*, 1915. Its perfect abstraction is that of decoration, and is atypical in the oeuvre. When Brancusi told the sculptor Isamu Noguchi that he "always started out from some recognizable image in nature,"[2] he was referring to his typical works; nor was he forgetting *Endless Column*, which belongs to another genre. Yet *Endless Column* is a decoration of the highest order, developing a new significance in every situation in which it is placed. The repetitions of its design and the variations in its execution surely link it to the opera *Socrate*, by Erik Satie, a close friend of the sculptor.

[1] P. G. Adrian, "Constantin Brancusi," *Goya*, January 1957.
[2] Isamu Noguchi, *A Sculptor's World*, New York, Harper and Row, 1968, p. 18.

CUP II

Wood, 7 3/8″ × 14 1/4″ × 11 5/8″
   (18.7 × 36.3 × 29.6 cm.), 1918?
Not inscribed
Collection Musée National d'Art Moderne, Paris; acquired
   1957 by bequest from the artist

No exhibitions

References
Geist no. 110
Pound, 1921, pl. 21 (unfinished)
M.M., 1923, p. 16

Cup II, unfinished, appears in *The Little Review*, 1921,
pl. 25, in a photograph probably taken at the end of 1917.
An earlier, smaller version which would seem to have
belonged to John Quinn, and two later, larger versions are
all in the Musée d'Art Moderne.

The order of increasing size appears to be the chronological
order of the versions of *Cup;* but they exhibit differences in
their proportions—*Cup II* has relatively the largest ear, only
Cup I is taller than *Cup II*—and *Cup III* has a square ear.
The main element of *Cup* is similar to the topmost element
of *Eve* which seems to precede it by a year.

By making a number of smaller changes with respect to
the everyday object—filling in the concavity, making the ear
solid, and rounding the bottom—Brancusi has re-created
the ideal form of the cup, and made a work emblematic of
his manner of conceiving the world.

After the *head as object* and the *torso as object, Cup* is
that unusual creation, the *object as object*. This charming
enterprise is surely related to *"musique d'ameublement"*
—"furniture music"—the casual background music invented
by Brancusi's friend, Erik Satie, at this same time. The work
has the alternate title of *Cup of Socrates;* among his friends
Satie was known as "Socrates."

Groupe Mobile? *wood, 1917*

HEAD

Wood, 12″ (30.5 cm.) long, 1920–23
Not inscribed
Collection Yolanda Penteado, São Paulo; acquired
  ca. 1950–52 from the artist

Exhibitions
Brummer Gallery, New York, 1933–34, no. 47
Guggenheim Museum, New York, 1955–56
  Philadelphia Museum, 1956

References
Geist no. 145
Pound, 1921, pls. 6, 7, 23 (full figure)
This Quarter, 1925, pl. 26, full figure
Zervos, 1957, p. 100

This head is all that remains of a second version of *Little French Girl*, shorter than the first and somewhat more simplified. The figure would seem to have been carved in 1919; it was still in existence in 1923.

Head is designed in bold elements and without the subtle detail of the first version. Brancusi has moved the eye to the left side; the head of first *Little French Girl*, *The Newborn* and the head of *The First Step* all had the eye on the right. Free of the body, this shape can only be read as an abstract construct.

Little French Girl II, *wood, 1919? destroyed*

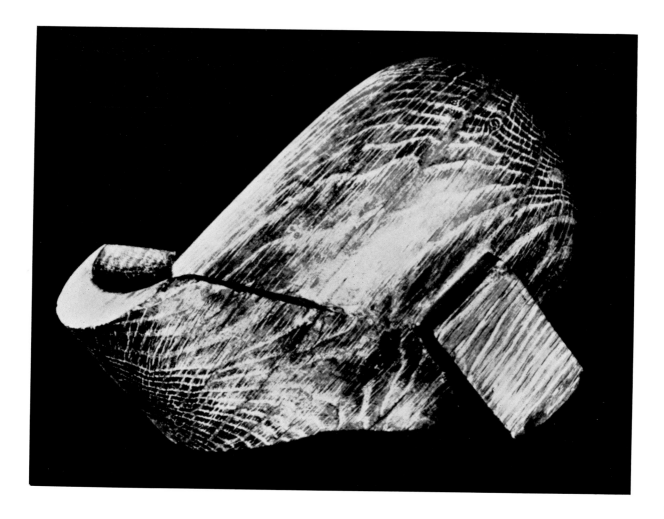

93

GOLDEN BIRD

Polished bronze, 36 1/2" (92.7 cm.) high, 1919
Inscribed: C Brancusi
Collection The Arts Club of Chicago; acquired 1927

Provenance
John Quinn, acquired 1920 from the artist

Exhibitions
Sculptor's Gallery, New York, 1922, no. 14
Brummer Gallery, New York, 1926, no. 20, pl. 20
    Arts Club of Chicago, 1927
University of Chicago, 1934, no. 3
City Art Museum of St. Louis, 1946, no. 81
Cincinnati Art Museum, 1946, no. 3
Philadelphia Museum, 1952
    Art Institute of Chicago, 1953, no. 10

References
Geist no. 117
Einstein, 1926, pl. 525
Einstein, 1931, pl. 618
Zervos, 1935, p. 96

Dated in the 1926 Brummer Gallery catalogue; acquired by
John Quinn in 1920. Another version in bronze is known.

Golden Bird is a bronze from *Yellow Bird*, marble, in the
Yale University Art Gallery, a work all but finished at the
end of 1917; it was broken soon after and repaired.

Previous examples of the *Bird* had been starkly rationalized
versions of the natural creature; here Brancusi takes
advantage of the gradual compression of parts caused by
elongation, and makes body, legs and feathers continuous.
In leaving behind the enumeration of anatomical features,
Yellow Bird represents a bold departure and one that sets
the stage for the final resolution—still some years off—of
this theme.

Golden Bird is perched on a dangerously small footing.
It rises in a gush of gleaming metal which is not only a new
image of the bird, but surely an expression of the sculptor's
thrill of discovery.

MLLE. POGANY II

Veined marble, 17 3/8 " (44.2 cm.) high, 1919
Inscribed: C Brâncuși
Collection Mr. and Mrs. Lee A. Ault, New York; acquired
    1941

Provenance
Pierre Matisse Gallery, New York, acquired 1940
Brummer Gallery, New York
John Quinn, acquired November 1920 from the artist

Exhibitions
31st Salon des Indépendants, Paris, 1920, not listed
Sculptor's Gallery, New York, 1922, no. 15
Brummer Gallery, New York, 1926, no. 24, pl. 24
    Arts Club of Chicago, 1927
Valentine Gallery, New York, 1944, no. 63, illus.
Guggenheim Museum, New York, 1955–56
Staempfli Gallery, New York, 1965
Perls Galleries, New York, 1966, no. 117

References
Geist no. 119
Pound, 1921, pls. 6, 9, 10, 11
Martel, 1929, pl. 10
Gertz, 1953, p. 169
Zervos, 1957, pp. 44, 47
Giedion-Welcker, 1959, pl. 28
Reid, 1968, after p. 430

Dated in the 1926 Brummer catalogue. Only one piece by
Brancusi, "Sculpture," is listed in the catalogue of the
Salon des Indépendants, Paris, January 28–February 29,
1920; this title must refer to *Princess X* which was removed
from the exhibition (see page 78). In view of these circum-
stances, it is surprising to learn, in a note dated February 1,
1920, from H. P. Roché to John Quinn, that *Mlle.
Pogany II* was in the exhibition, where Roché had just
seen it.

Carved seven years after the first version, *Mlle. Pogany II*
simplifies and condenses the design, taking advantage of
elements which appeared in *Danaïde*. The eyeball is not
rendered but is absorbed now by the cheek, a sweeping
eyelid showing its upper limit. The slit of the mouth is
absent; the two arms merge in a single large form; the
earlier coiled bun of hair has become a cascade of arches
ending in a whorl a short distance above the base. With the
mass of the shoulder removed, the bottom of the work has
an area of barely three square inches.

   In spite of its new sumptuousness of *matière* and many
changes in the direction of pure design, the height of the
work remains constant. The force of personality of the
original is diminished, but has not disappeared.

MLLE. POGANY II

Polished bronze, 17" (43.2 cm.) high, 1920
Inscribed: C. Brâncuşi [and on base] 1920
Collection Albright-Knox Art Gallery, Buffalo, New York
   Charlotte A. Watson Fund, 1927

Provenance
John Quinn, acquired November 1920 from the artist

Exhibitions
Sculptor's Gallery, New York, 1922, no. 16
Brummer Gallery, New York, 1926, no. 19, pl. 19
   Arts Club of Chicago, 1927
Art Gallery of Toronto, 1927, illus. p. 10
Brummer Gallery, New York, 1933–34, no. 58
Albright Art Gallery, Buffalo, 1936, no. 126
Museum of Modern Art, New York, 1942–43, illus. p. 68
Cincinnati Art Museum, 1946, no. 2
Baltimore Museum of Art, 1948, no. 24, illus.
Minneapolis Institute of Arts, 1949, illus.
Philadelphia Museum of Art, 1952
   Art Institute of Chicago, 1953, no. 11
   Museum of Modern Art, New York, 1953, no. 11
Museum of Fine Arts, Houston, 1953, no. 27, illus.
   Museum of Modern Art, New York, 1953, no. 11
Museum of Fine Arts, Boston, 1957, no. 16
XXX Biennale, Venice, 1960, no. 7

References
Geist no. 120a
Pound, 1921, pls. 1–6, 8, 9, 24
Einstein, 1926, pl. XXXVIII
Ritchie, 1952, p. 109
Zervos, 1957, p. 45
Giedion-Welcker, 1959, pl. 29

In the Brancusi number of *The Little Review*, 1921, this
work appears in ten illustrations. There are two other casts,
made at a later date.

The advanced stylization of the marble is brought to an
absolute point in the metal version. High polish renders the
image abstract and swift. It is now a trap for light, a
glistening construct of shifting reflections.

DANAIDE

Polished bronze, except hair, 10 5/8" (27 cm.) high, 1913?
Inscribed: C. BRANCUSI
Collection Philadelphia Museum of Art,
    Bequest of Mrs. S. S. White, 1967

Provenance
Mrs. S. S. White
Earl Horter

Exhibitions
Philadelphia Museum, 1950

References
Geist no. 73e
Jianou, 1963, pl. 102
Philadelphia Museum Bulletin, January–March /
    April–June, 1968, pl. 2

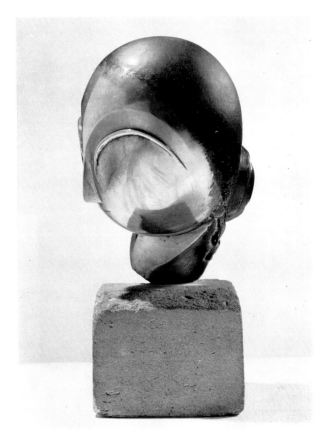

DANAIDE

Polished bronze, 11" (28 cm.) high, 1913?
Inscribed: C Brâncusi
Collection Mrs. G. H. Warren, New York; acquired 1944
    at auction

Provenance
Mr. and Mrs. Maurice Speiser, from the artist

Exhibitions
Knoedler Gallery, New York, 1949, no. 23

References
Geist no. 73f

The original marble of this work was shown at the Gallery of the Photo-Secession, New York, in March 1914. It was reworked in 1925, the main change being the elimination of the facial features so as to present a continuous surface. This reworked head is the *Head of a Woman* in the collection of Mr. and Mrs. Isadore Levin, Detroit; its height is 11 1/8″.

Six bronzes have been recorded which depend from the marble, three having a height of 10 5/8″, three having a height much closer, or equal, to that of the marble. Of the shorter casts (where the loss of height occurs in the neck) two were partly gilded, and one covered with a black patina; one of the former was exhibited in the Photo-Secession exhibition. Of the taller casts, two of which are in the exhibition, one is partly polished and the other is completely polished; a third, in The Tate Gallery, London, was probably polished; one of these was published in *The Little Review*, 1921. These differences in size, and appearance in an exhibition or publication, make it seem that the shorter versions were cast not later than 1913, the taller in 1920. But it does not seem likely—in 1913, two years after polishing *Maiastra* and *Prometheus*, and the same year when large areas of *Mlle. Pogany* were polished—that Brancusi would have left *Danaïde* unpolished. I am therefore proposing that the first three casts were made in 1910, that is, before the bronze of *Maiastra*, and that the marble was carved the same year, the year in which Brancusi met Margit Pogany. According to a memoir by Mlle. Pogany, Brancusi made a study of her from memory, which I believe to be *Danaïde*. In about 1952 the sculptor told Dr. Heinz Keller, Zurich, that it was a preliminary stage of *Mlle. Pogany*, 1912; Athena T. Spear, Oberlin, Ohio, contends, for stylistic reasons, that it postdates *Mlle. Pogany*.

Danaïde, for the present writer, falls stylistically between the lost *Narcissus* and *Prometheus*. With respect to *Mlle. Pogany* it would then seem to be a premature development, one that Brancusi would not assimilate until the *Mlle. Pogany II* of 1919. Like *Prometheus*, it goes in the direction of pure design, a residue of personality saving it from being a mere exercise.

Narcissus, *alabaster? 1910? lost*

Danaide, *marble, 1910, recarved*

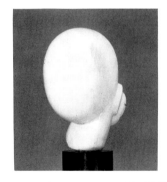

Head of a Woman, *marble, 1925, coll. Mr. and Mrs. Isidore Levin, Detroit*

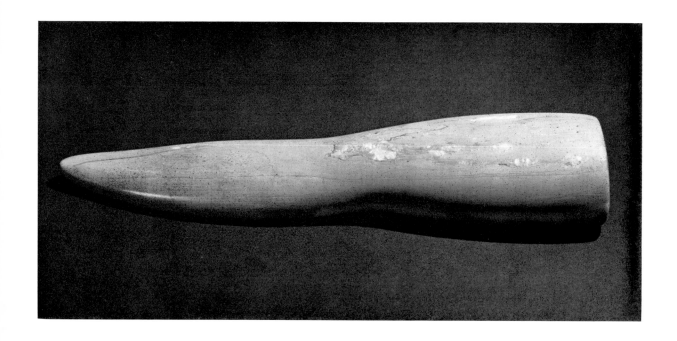

A HAND

Yellow marble, 12″ (30.35 cm.) long, 1920
Inscribed: C. Brâncuși à John Quinn Paris 1920
        BRANCUSI a ME HARE NEW-YORK 1926
Collection The Fogg Art Museum, Harvard University,
    Cambridge, Massachusetts, Gift of Mr. and Mrs. Max
    Wasserman, 1964

Provenance
Mrs. Meredith Hare, acquired 1926
John Quinn, acquired 1921, gift from the artist

Exhibitions
Sculptor's Gallery, New York, 1922, no. 18
Carpenter Center for Visual Arts, Harvard University, 1966

References
Geist no. 130
Geist, 1964, p. 71

In a letter to John Quinn, dated December 7, 1920,
Brancusi wrote: "I have also sent you in the same group, to
complete the collection and in the hope of pleasing you,
three small things which I beg you to accept from me
without payment—they are: a drawing, a study for Mlle.
Pogany—a cup in wood which you might keep in your
dining room—and a little hand in colored marble which you
may keep on your desk—it is with great pleasure that I offer
them to you."

A Hand is carved in a piece of marble similar to that of the
previous *Yellow Bird*; a plane across the underside keeps
the object stable. The image is reminiscent of the hand in
A Muse and *Mlle. Pogany*. But *A Hand* is not simply a
version of an anatomical member: it suggests—and invites—
a caress.

LEDA

Marble, 21″ (23.3 cm.) high, 1920
Collection The Art Institute of Chicago, Bequest of
    Katherine S. Dreier Estate

Provenance
Katherine S. Dreier, aquired by 1936

Exhibitions
Brooklyn Museum, New York, 1926–27, no. 164
Museum of Modern Art, New York, 1936, no. 19, illus.
    Cleveland Museum of Art, 1937
Yale University Art Gallery, New Haven, 1952–53, no. 4
Guggenheim Museum New York, 1955–56

References
Geist no. 131
The Little Review, 1921, pl. 14
This Quarter, 1925, pl. 24
Fierens, 1933, pl. 23
Zervos, 1957, pl. 76
Lewis, 1957, pl. 37
Giedion-Welcker, 1959, psl. 50, 51
Jianou, 1963, fig. 39

The work is reproduced in *The Little Review*, 1921, pl. 14.
It was dated 1920 in the exhibition "Cubism and Abstract
Art" at The Museum of Modern Art, New York, 1936. There
is a version in bronze at the Musée d'Art Moderne, Paris.

Leda appears to be round-bottomed and precariously
balanced. The upper element projects dangerously from the
lower mass and has a very small area of attachment to it
(and has broken at this point).
The image is difficult to read. And *Leda* is one of the most
intriguing of Brancusi's creations. The charm of *Leda* is, of
course, largely composed of its problems.
    Leda was originally on a base that revolved slowly;
movement compensated for the fact that the lateral extension of the work often kept it from being intelligible.
    Of *Leda* Brancusi said, "It is Leda, not Jupiter, changing
into a swan." At the same time that Brancusi creates his
own myth he creates—in this passive ovoidal form penetrated
by the more clearly structured element—an image that must
relate to any fable of Leda: an image of fertilization.

KING OF KINGS

Oak, 118 1/8" (3.0 m.) high, 1920?
Not inscribed
Collection The Solomon R. Guggenheim Museum, New York;
    acquired 1956 from the artist

Exhibitions
Guggenheim Museum, New York, 1955–56
    Philadelphia Museum, 1956
XXX Biennale, Venice, 1960, no. 5, illus. pl. 47
Arts Club of Chicago, 1960, no. 6, illus.

References
Geist no. 127
Zervos, 1957, p. 60
Lewis, 1957, pl. 27
Liberman, 1960, pl. 81
Jianou, 1963, pl. 66

This work was done for a "Temple of Meditation" projected
in 1933 for the Maharajah of Indore, according to Giedion-
Giedion-Welcker, 1959, p. 35. After a visit to Indore at the
very end of 1937; Brancusi realized the temple would not be
built. However this may be, the work is mentioned by no
one until after the end of the second World War; Marcel
Duchamp suggested to the author that it was done about
1920. The sculptor Constantin Antonovici, New York, who
assisted Brancusi in the period 1947–51, removed some
wood from the upper part of the work in 1949. At the time
Brancusi said, "It is never finished."

Brancusi's largest indoor sculpture, *King of Kings* seems to
anthologize the favorite forms and motifs of his sculpture
in wood, though we note the absence of the truncated
pyramids which compose *Endless Column*, and the inclusion
of a helical shape, unique in the oeuvre. Cohesion here is
supplied by verticality, containment within the confines of a
beam, and a general figural quality. Though the two upper
elements have the appearance of a head and a flame-like
crown, Brancusi may have attempted a version of a Tibetan
Ch'orten which symbolizes in ascending order: earth, water,
fire, air, ether. He originally referred to the work as *Spirit of
Buddha*, but changed the title to its present one, an allusion
to Genghis Khan. The head has a forbidding character; the
openings are as disturbing here as the one in *Chimera*. In
1948 Brancusi told Mrs. Calvert Coggeshall, New York, that
he was not satisfied with the work.

    Though *King of Kings* presents problems, it is at once
reserved and authoritative, a masterly orchestration of
difficult materials, absolute in its design despite its ease of
execution.

The Tibetan Ch'orten

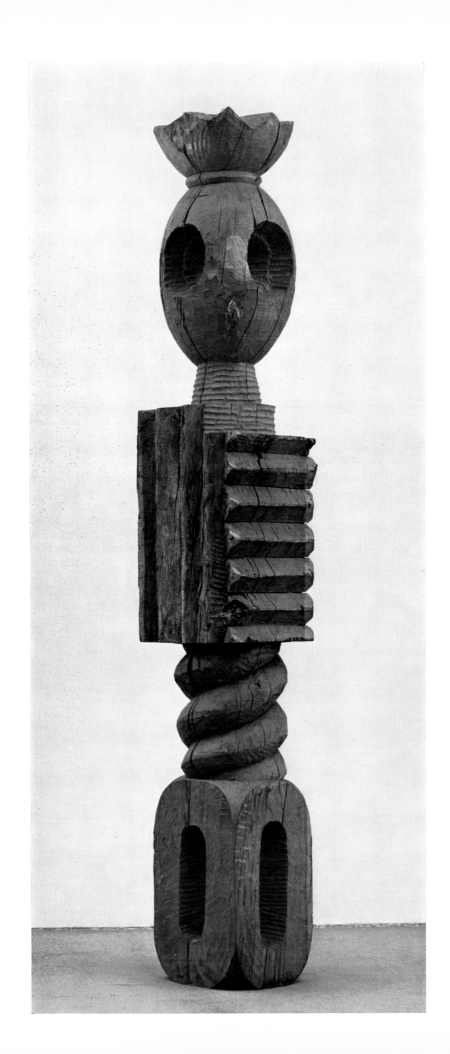

ADAM AND EVE

Oak, chestnut, limestone, 94 1/4" (2.394 m.), 1916–1921
Inscribed: CB [three times]
EVE
Oak, 46 1/4" (118.1 cm.) high, 1916–1919
ADAM
Chestnut, 34 7/8" (88.6 cm.) high, 1917
Collection The Solomon R. Guggenheim Museum,
   New York, 1953

Provenance
H. P. Roché
John Quinn, acquired 1922 from the artist

Exhibitions
Brummer Gallery, New York, 1926, nos. 17, 18, pls. 17, 18
   Arts Club of Chicago, 1927
Sidney Janis Gallery, New York, 1951
Musée National d'Art Moderne, Paris, 1952, no. 117
   Tate Gallery, London, 1952, no. 98
Guggenheim Museum, New York, 1955–56
   Philadelphia Museum, 1956
XXX Biennale, Venice, 1960, p. 33, no. 8, illus.
The Jewish Museum, New York, 1963, no. 11, illus.

References
Geist no. 134
M. M., 1923, pp. 18, 19, 22; *Eve*, p. 23
Fierens, 1933, pl. 21 (*Eve* alone)
Ritchie, 1952, p. 114
Zervos, 1957, p. 67
Read, 1956, pls. 216 and 217
Giedion-Welcker, 1959, pls. 82, 83, 84
Jianou, 1963, pl. 63
Marchiori, 1963, pl. 4
De Micheli, 1966, pl. X

In the Brancusi Bequest at the Musée d'Art Moderne, Paris, is a photograph of the completed *Eve*, in its early state, together with the roughed-out *Sorceress*, begun 1916; and a photograph of *Eve* alone is dated 1916 by the artist. *Adam* is dated 1917 in Giedion-Welcker 1959, p. 152. The present state of *Eve* alone is dated both 1920 and 1922 in *This Quarter*, 1925. *Adam and Eve* is dated 1921 in the 1926 Brummer catalogue.

Before the recent discovery of the photographs of *Eve* among Brancusi's effects it had not been suspected that the work had had another state (page 80). In this state its eroticism and debt to primitive art are even more emphatic than at present. The creation of *Eve* in Paris in 1916 is inconceivable without knowledge of African art, regardless of whether Brancusi actually knew the Bambara marionette figures with which it has surprising affinities. It is now apparent that with *Princess X* and *The Sorceress* it is part of a constellation of female images related in time and by an unexpected attention to the motif of breasts. Sublimated in *The Sorceress*, this motif is suppressed in *Adam and Eve* by an actual reduction of the forms, by their placement on a large block whose mass and profile minimize theirs, and by the absorption of *Eve* into a larger complex.

   Adam by itself is an ambiguous image, now figure, now base; and, in a telegram to John Quinn in 1922, H. P. Roché refers to it as "Adambase," an appellation it probably did not acquire before its association with *Eve*.

   Adam and Eve, like several other works by Brancusi, is achieved by a superposition of parts, a mode of organization common to primitive sculpture. In bringing together, long after they were carved, two objects in different styles, Brancusi demonstrates a decorative gift, since it was no simple matter to adjust these pieces to each other. But the task also required a certain faith in the unconscious processes of his imagination. The work surely reflects Brancusi's current attitude on the social relations of the sexes: beautiful woman is now the crushing burden of responsible man. We have come a long way from the idyllic equality of *The Kiss*.

Torso of a Young Woman, *onyx, 1918, coll. Mme. Denise
Roché, Sèvres, France*

TORSO OF A GIRL II

Onyx, 12 3/4″ (32.5 cm.) high, 1922?
Not inscribed
Collection Philadelphia Museum of Art,
    A. E. Gallatin Collection, 1952

Provenance
A. E. Gallatin, acquired between 1933 and 1937

Exhibitions
Brummer Gallery, New York, 1933–34, no. 21
Museum of Living Art, New York, 1937, no. 11, illus.
Philadelphia Museum, 1954, no. 15, illus. p. 68
Guggenheim Museum, New York, 1955–56
    Philadelphia Museum, 1956

References
Geist no. 140
The Art News, 1933, p. 6
Martin, 1937, pl. 25
Lewis, 1957, pl. 36
Giedion-Welcker, 1959, pl. 33
Jianou, 1963, pl. 54
Licht, 1967, pl. 190

Another version of this motif, now in a private collection, was acquired by John Quinn in 1922. The present work would seem to have been carved between this date and 1925, the date of a third version in the Musée d'Art Moderne, Paris.

Torso of a Girl is a radical stylization of the more realistic *Torso of a Young Woman*, 1918. Brancusi has retained the plane at the top and the projection of the buttocks at the rear, but in eliminating the pubic area and the legs he has made an ambiguous image of the female pelvic region, identifiable by its title and derivation rather than by its form. The work now suggests a precariously balanced container—the womb. It is thus a typical Brancusian transformation of an earlier work: from an image specific in its reference the sculptor extracts another that transcends it by forcing the design in the direction of greater abstraction.

The spirit of this work and of *Torso of a Young Woman*, 1918, from which it derives, differs sharply from that of the preceding wood carvings and, most importantly, of *Timidity*, 1917, another image of the pelvic region. In returning to the relative naturalism of the *Torso* of 1918, Brancusi questions the primitivising, even africanising, vision of the previous years. This vision found expression for the most part in works in wood; Brancusi reserves a more European vision for the paler, reflective marble and onyx.

Torso of a Girl, *onyx, 1922, private coll.*

Torso of a Girl III, *marble, 1925, coll. Musée National d'Art Moderne, Paris*

FISH

Veined marble, 5″ × 16 7/8″ × 13/16″
   (12.7 × 42.9 × 2.0 cm.), on a circular mirror,
   17″ (43.0 cm.) diam., 1922
Not inscribed
Collection Philadelphia Museum of Art,
   The Louise and Walter Arensberg Collection; by bequest,
   1950

Provenance
Walter Arensberg, acquired 1948
Earl Stendahl, acquired 1946
John Quinn, acquired 1923

Exhibitions
Brummer Gallery, New York, 1926, no. 13, pl. 13
   Arts Club of Chicago, 1927
Cincinnati Art Museum, 1946, no. 5
City Art Museum of St. Louis, 1946, no. 78
Art Institute of Chicago, 1949, no. 18, illus.
Philadelphia Museum, 1954, no. 16, illus.
Guggenheim Museum, New York, 1955–56
   Philadelphia Museum, 1956

References
Geist no. 141
Zervos, 1957, p. 71
Lewis, 1957, pl. 45
Jianou, 1963, pl. 52

Dated by the listing in the 1926 Brummer catalogue.

If *Timidity* is at one extreme of Brancusi's symmetrical
works, *Fish* is at the other; when viewed along its plane of
symmetry it all but disappears. The critic Robert Pincus-
Witten has observed that when seen from above, against its
disk, it makes a design like that of the eye of late versions
of *The Kiss*.

   Fish has several surprising new features: it is perfectly
unstable; it is the first of the fixed sculptures to explore
horizontality; its physical substance is meager; it is not
simply an object, but the occupant of a situation created by
a circular disk and its reflection.

   The work has the absolute simplicity of a deep innocence.
Yet despite its purity and seeming paucity of data, the
profile is calculated to register constantly changing
information.

   Fish bears the responsibility in the last two decades of
having spawned a numberless school of sculptured fish;
but their ornamental nature only serves to underline the
seriousness of Brancusi.

EILEEN

Marble, 11 1/4″ (28.7 cm.) high, 1923?
Not inscribed
Collection Musée National d'Art Moderne, Paris; acquired
  1957 by bequest of the artist

Exhibitions
Brummer Gallery, New York, 1933–34, no. 51

References
Geist no. 157
Liberman, 1960, pl. 83
Geist, Oct. 1964, p. 54

The work is difficult to date, but since Brancusi met the
model around 1922, it is likely that he carved it near the
beginning of their friendship.

Eileen was inspired by the young woman who accompanied
the sculptor on a trip to Rumania in 1922. She had black
hair which she wore in a tight bun on the back of her head,
and in showing this one distinctive feature, Brancusi created
his most simplified portrait.

   The very reductive image is not a "free form." We sense a
strict construction around a vertical axis which rises at the
point where head and base meet; the bulge of the bun is
around an axis perpendicular to the longer one. The sculpture shifts easily from representation to pure form.

FISH

Polished bronze, 5″ × 16 7/8″ 1 × 1/8″
   (12.7 × 42.9 × 2.9 cm.), 1924
Inscribed: N.1 C. BRÂNCUŞI-PARIS-1924
   [printed with punches]
Collection Mr. and Mrs. James W. Alsdorf, Winnetka,
   Illinois, 1968

Provenance
Private Collection, New York
Mrs. Hilda C. Rodman
Maynard Walker Gallery, New York
Mrs. Meredith Hare
Mrs. Charles Rumsey, acquired from the artist

Exhibitions
New Chenil Galleries, London, 1925, no. 3
Brummer Gallery, New York, 1926, no. 14, pl. 14
   Arts Club of Chicago, 1927
Guggenheim Museum, New York, 1955–56
   Philadelphia Museum, 1956
Staempfli Gallery, New York, 1960, no. 11

References
Geist no. 147
This Quarter, 1925, pl. 23
Einstein, 1931, pl. 621
Giedion-Welcker, 1959, pl. 66

Of approximately the same height and length as the marble
Fish from which it derives, the bronze increases in thickness
by almost a third, a modification achieved in an intermediate
plaster. Brancusi mounts the metal *Fish* on a conventional
base abandoning the reflective disk of the original. This
spare gleaming object carries the idea of fish to an extreme
of abstraction.
   Brancusi told the American sculptor Malvina Hoffman
that he did not want to do a fish but "the flash of its spirit."

BEGINNING OF THE WORLD

Polished bronze 11 1/4″ (28.6 cm.) long, 1924?
Not inscribed
Base by the artist
Collection Musée National d'Art Moderne, Paris; acquired
    1957 by bequest from the artist

No exhibitions

References
Geist no. 148
Liberman, 1960, pl. 82

The work is a version of *Beginning of the World*, marble
(Geist no. 132) which this writer dates 1920.

If *Sculpture for the Blind* was a muted or effaced version of
a human head, *Beginning of the World* carried the process
of abstraction further to become an egg of creation. The
planar construction evident in the marble all but disappears
in the polished bronze. This taut, gleaming object is a golden
egg of creation, presaging a new metallic universe—
impersonal, weightless, light-filled.

THE KISS

Brown stone, 14 3/8″ × 10 1/8″ × 9 1/2″
   (36.6 × 25.6 × 24.1 cm.), 1925
Inscribed: C. Brancus PARIS 1925 34
Collection Musée National d'Art Moderne, Paris; acquired
   1957 by bequest from the artist

Exhibitions
Brummer Gallery, New York, 1933–34, no. 34

References
Geist no. 135
This Quarter, 1925, pl. 11
Vitrac, 1929, p. 392
Einstein, 1931, pl. 623
Jianou, 1963, pl. 4
Brezianu, 1969, pl. 6

The inscription "34" refers to the listing of the work in the 1933–34 Brummer Gallery catalogue.

The Kiss in brown stone, with its very shallow relief and rounded heads, is the most compact and massive of the six versions of this theme; it appears at a time when Brancusi makes other works which are equally compact. The encircling arms of earlier versions here pass each other, in subtle fashions the continuity of the mass is delicately broken by the changing surface, now impersonally smooth, now starred by the marks of the bush hammer. The eyes on one side of the heads lie on the general plane; on the other side they bulge above it. In this late version of a favorite theme sexual distinction has all but vanished.

WHITE NEGRESS

Veined marble, 15″ (38.1 cm.) high, 1923
Not inscribed
Collection Philadelphia Museum of Art,
    The Louise and Walter Arensberg Collection; by bequest,
    1950

Provenance
Walter Arensberg, acquired ca. 1932

Exhibitions
Wildenstein Galleries, New York, 1926
Art Institute of Chicago, 1949, no. 16
Philadelphia Museum, 1954, no. 17, illus.
Guggenheim Museum, New York, 1955–56
    Philadelphia Museum, 1956

References
Geist no. 149
This Quarter, 1925, pls. 16, 26
Martel, 1929, pl. 10
Zervos, 1957, p. 75
Lewis, 1957, pl. 40
Giedion-Welcker, 1959, pl. 18
Jianou, 1963, pl. 57

Dated by inclusion in pl. 26 of *This Quarter*, 1925, where *Bird in Space* (Geist no. 146) is visible. The sculptor delivered this *Bird in Space* to his packer on December 10, 1923, for shipment to John Quinn.

The recumbent ovoid that was *Beginning of the World*, and that itself derived from a sleeping head, is here transformed into an ellipsoid placed on its long axis to be the central element of a new head, erect and alert. To this element are added three small forms of which two are familiar: the lips resemble the lower half of the head of *Eve*, the ornament at the rear resembles the flamelike motif of *King of Kings*. The addition of three forms to another, without modulation or transition, appears to be an effort to constitute a head by a *constellation* of elements, a new venture for an artist who up to this point has practiced compression and reduction. *White Negress* was inspired by a young African woman whom Brancusi met at an official reception.

BIRD IN SPACE

Polished bronze, 50″ (127 cm.) high, 1924
Inscribed: C. Brancusi
Collection Philadelphia Museum of Art,
    The Louise and Walter Arensberg Collection; by bequest,
    1950

Provenance
Walter Arensberg, acquired ca. 1927

Exhibitions
Wildenstein Galleries, New York, 1926
Art Institute of Chicago, 1949, no. 15
Philadelphia Museum, 1952, no. 12
Philadelphia Museum, 1954, no. 19, illus.
Guggenheim Museum, New York, 1955–56
    Philadelphia Museum, 1956
Museum of Fine Arts, Boston, 1957, no. 17
Cleveland Museum of Art, 1966, no. 34

References
Geist no. 150
Lewis, 1957, pl. 55
Jianou, 1963, pl. 48
Goldwater, 1967, p. 32

The work postdates the Marx-Schoenborn *Bird in Space*, 1923, sent to John Quinn in December of that year.

The body of this first bronze *Bird in Space* is a variation of the body of the marble *Bird* that preceded it; its footing is a variation of the same feature in a transitional plaster *Bird* (Geist no. 142). That a slender footing, which approximates Brancusi's later design of this feature, should first appear in metal leads us to suppose that Brancusi was not yet able to execute it in marble. At any rate it is clear from his letter of December 18, 1923, to John Quinn that the footing of the preceding marble (coll. Marx-Schoenborn) had caused him trouble: "I sent you the sculptures a little later than I would have wished—I delayed on account of the bottom of the bird which I had to study a great deal."

This *Bird in Space*, while lacking the grace of Brancusi's later versions, is nevertheless of a piece, its energy preliminary to the suavity of the *Birds* that would follow it.

Bird in Space, *marble, 1923,*
Marx-Schoenborn coll., New York

114

BIRD IN SPACE

Yellow marble, 45 3/4" (116.2 cm.) high, 1925
Inscribed: C. Brancusi
Collection Philadelphia Museum of Art,
    The Louise and Walter Arensberg Collection; by bequest,
    1950

Provenance
Walter Arensberg, acquired 1949
Stendahl Galleries, Hollywood
Curt Valentin, New York

Exhibitions
Brummer Gallery, New York, 1926, no. 37
    Arts Club of Chicago, 1927
Philadelphia Museum, 1952, no. 13
Philadelphia Museum, 1954, no. 20, illus.
Guggenheim Museum, New York, 1955–56
    Philadelphia Museum, 1956

References
Geist no. 154
This Quarter, 1925, pl. 9
Lewis, 1957, pl. 54
Jianou, 1963, pl. 47

Dated in the 1926 Brummer catalogue. The footing has
been broken and repaired, probably by the sculptor.

This *Bird in Space* is the first example of Brancusi's final
resolution of this theme, one that from this point to 1941
will have thirteen variations. The technical problem of boring
a hole for the internal metal rod apparently was not solved;
the footing shattered and was repaired in an obvious fashion.
For so delicate a design it is curious that Brancusi did not
use a marble of more even grain.

But evident here, very soon after the previous version in a
different spirit, is Brancusi's image of dream flight, rising
with a grace and ease that leave behind its own heavy
matter.

PORTRAIT OF NANCY CUNARD

Wood, 20 3/8″ (54.3 cm.) high, 1925
Not inscribed
Private Collection; acquired from the artist

Exhibitions
Brummer Gallery, New York, 1933, no. 36
Guggenheim Museum, New York, 1955–56
Staempfli Gallery, New York, 1960, no. 8, illus.

References
Geist no. 160
Giedion-Welcker, 1959, pl. 53

Dated 1925 by the inscription, 1925–28, on a plaster of the
later version in bronze. The subject was the beautiful and
daring poet and patron of poets, a memorable personality
of the twenties. Brancusi, along with George Moore, was
her guest at a Christmas eve dinner at La Rotonde in
Paris in 1923; it is not likely that he saw much of her after
this occasion though she was associated for a while with
the poet, Tristan Tzara, a Rumanian and a friend of his and it
was not till many years later that Miss Cunard became aware
that Brancusi had done a head which bore her name. The
work has the alternate title: *Sophisticated Young Lady*.

If *The Chief* makes its point largely by the removal of a seg-
ment from a fully developed form, in the *Nancy Cunard*
Brancusi, in opposite fashion, adds one form to another.
(The central form of the sculpture is similar to *Little Bird*
turned on its head.) In both cases the device is extreme, and
the effect surprising and humorous. Both works make a
sharp social commentary.

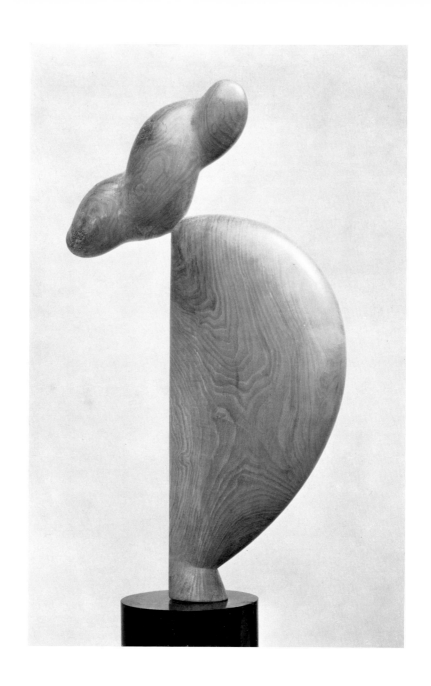

LITTLE BIRD

Colored marble, 16 1/4" (41.2 cm.) high, 1925
Inscribed: C. branCUSI Paris 1925
Collection Norton Simon Museum of Art Inc., Fullerton,
California; acquired 1968.

Provenance
R. Sturgis Ingersoll, Penllyn, Pennsylvania; acquired
  ca. 1927 from the artist.

Exhibitions
Wildenstein Galleries, New York, 1926
Salon des Tuileries, Paris, 1926, no. 252
Philadelphia Museum of Art, 1933
Brummer Gallery, New York, 1933–34, no. 1
Philadelphia Museum of Art, 1950
Philadelphia Museum of Art, 1956
The Washington Gallery of Modern Art, 1963, no. 7, illus.

References
Geist no. 161
Lewis, 1957, pl. 47
Zervos, 1957, p. 73
Giedion-Welcker, 1959, pl. 34

There is a version in bronze. The title in French is *L'Oiselet*;
another version in marble is titled *Young Bird* in the
catalogue of the 1933–34 Brummer exhibition.

Little Bird is formally related to both the central feature of
Portrait of Nancy Cunard and *Torso of a Girl*. With its
important gaping mouth and heavy body it represents the
fledgling state of *Bird in Space*, lacking as it does the undulating footing which suggests the motive power of the
large bird. It has the spine of the latter, of whose body it is
indeed a compressed version.

   Brancusi has here informed a shape of great purity with
his own vision of the world. *Little Bird* demonstrates that
the creatures of his imagination may have offspring.

FISH

Polished bronze, 5″ × 16 1/2″ × 13/16″
   (17.7 × 41.9 × 2.1 cm.), on metal disk, 19 5/8″
   (50.0 cm.) diam., 1926?
Not inscribed
Collection Sidney Janis Gallery, New York

Provenance
Theodore Schempp and Knoedler Gallery from Galerie
   Charpentier at auction

Exhibitions
Sidney Janis Gallery, New York, 1960, no. 8, illus.
Sidney Janis Gallery, New York, 1961, no. 6, illus.
Sidney Janis Gallery, New York, March 1964
Sidney Janis Gallery, New York, November 1964, illus. pl. 2
Sidney Janis Gallery, New York, 1966
Cleveland Museum of Art, 1966, no. 35
Sidney Janis Gallery, New York, 1969

References
Geist no. 168 c

The work is dated by another bronze in the collection of
Mrs. Samuel Bronfman, Toronto.

Two years after mounting a bronze *Fish* on a marble cylinder,
Brancusi decides to mount new versions on polished chrome
steel disks. These are thinner and stronger (and of greater
diameter) than the mirror he used for the marble of 1922;
they have the additional virtue of not tarnishing. Their
silvery color sets off perfectly the golden forms above them,
and makes the proper metallic suggestion of water.
   Of the five bronze *Fish* which Brancusi made after the
marble, this example is closest to the original, having the
same height and thickness, and being only slightly shorter
in length.

FISH

Polished bronze, 4 1/2″ × 16 1/2″ × 1 3/16″
  (11.4 × 41.9 × 3.0 cm.), 1926?
Not inscribed
Collection Museum of Fine Arts, Boston,
  William Francis Warden Fund, 1957

Provenance
H. S. Ede, Cambridge, England, acquired from the artist
  before 1930

Exhibitions
New Burlington Galleries, London, 1936, no. 35
Museum of Fine Arts, Boston, 1957, no. 18

References
Geist no. 168 d
Lewis, 1957, pl. 44
Jianou, 1963, pl. 51
De Micheli, 1966, pl. VIII

Dated like the previous example.

If the Alsdorf *Fish* increased considerably the thickness of
the marble, the Boston example adds two millimeters to
this dimension and is the thickest of all versions of this
theme. Another (coll. Power, London) is the shortest; the
Janis *Fish* is the closest to the marble, which is the longest.

The present *Fish* is *relatively* the longest since the
height has been reduced a half inch, or twenty percent,
and the roundest because of its thickness. On another
version (coll. Bronfman, Toronto) Brancusi has increased
the height a half inch, making it relatively the shortest. It is
a revealing exercise to lower and raise these heights,
respectively, another half inch: the resulting shapes are not
Brancusian. The Absolute may not be definitive, but
Brancusi has explored its limits.

THE NEWBORN II

Stainless steel, 9 3/4″ (24.8 cm.) long, on polished metal
  disk, 17 3/4″ (45.0 cm.) diam., 1928?
Not inscribed
Collection Musée National d'Art Moderne, Paris; acquired
  1957 by bequest from the artist

Exhibitions
Brummer Gallery, New York, 1933–34, no. 32

References
Geist no. 122a

This work, which depends from a version in marble (coll.
Moderna Museet, Stockholm), is dated tentatively to follow
a version in bronze dated 1925 (Vitrac, 1929, p. 393) and
Brancusi's use, in 1926, of a stainless steel disk as a mount
for the bronze *Fish*.

The only sculpture of Brancusi's in this intractable metal is
further evidence of his mastery of materials. The formal
clarity and fulsome drawing had already been achieved in
the marble (itself influenced by the bronze of 1915). What
is new here is the curious tension between the coldness of
the medium and the perfection of execution on the one
hand, and the always affecting image on the other.

WHITE NEGRESS II

Marble, 15 7/8" (40.3 cm.) high, 1928
Inscribed: C. Brancusi 1928 [on cylinder]
Collection The Art Institute of Chicago; acquired 1967

Provenance
Helena Rubinstein, acquired from the artist

References
Geist no. 173
Spear, 1966, pl. 9

Two casts in bronze are known.

In a second version of *White Negress*, the height has
increased only slightly, but the chignon at the top is smooth
on both sides and more nearly circular, its axis continues
that of the head rather than being bent forward, and its
plane of symmetry lies along that of the head. The ornament
at the rear is thinner and more fragile than formerly; the
whole head is mounted further forward on the cylindrical
base. The unfigured marble, the new rigor, the perfection of
form show the influence of the preceding bronze.

In this version of an earlier work both the number and
delicacy of the changes and their remarkable effect on the
image are further evidence of the intensity of Brancusi's
research.

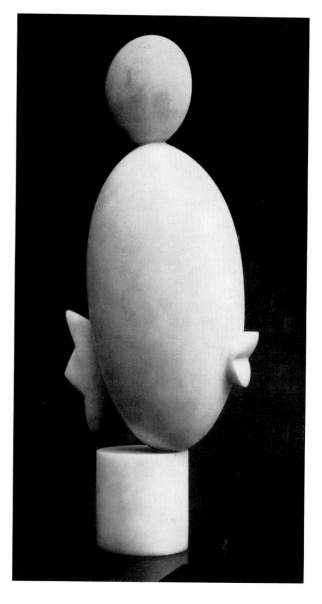

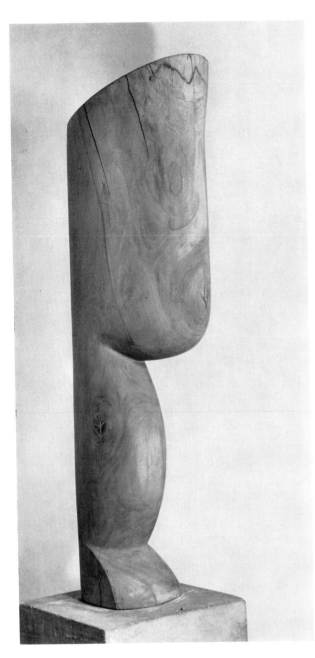

STUDY FOR PORTRAIT OF MRS. MEYER

Wood, 33" (83.8 cm.) high, 1916–1930?
Inscribed: 17 C Brancusi PARIS 1916
Collection Musée National d'Art Moderne, Paris; acquired
   1957 by bequest of the artist

Exhibitions
Brummer Gallery, New York, 1933–34, no. 17

References
Geist no. 176
This Quarter, 1925, pl. 15 (unfinished)
Geist, Oct. 1964, p. 55

The inscription "17" refers to the number of this work in
the 1933–34 Brummer Gallery catalogue. Although
inscribed "1916," the work was still in a roughed-out state
in 1925 (Geist, 1968, frontispiece). In 1948 the sculptor
told Mrs. C. Coggeshall, New York, that it was completed
after the marble *Portrait of Mrs. Eugene Meyer, Jr.*, 1930.

Brancusi was introduced to Mrs. Meyer by Edward Steichen
in 1912. She and her husband were instrumental in bringing
his sculpture to New York in 1914 for his first one-man
exhibition; it was at their home in the winter of 1926 that
he carved the pedestal for her *Bird in Space;* they eventually
acquired five examples of his sculpture. Neither the *Study*
nor the work in marble was commissioned.

   Whereas Brancusi usually translated carvings into versions
in bronze, the *Mrs. Meyer* is the unique case in the oeuvre
of a conception in wood inspiring a similar version in
marble.

   The *Study* was begun in a period when Brancusi was
much influenced by African Negro sculpture. It was a period,
too, in which he was exploring the matter of equilibrium:
the projection of the head tempts the overturning point and
creates a profile which is the more surprising when read
against the perfectly straight back. The work is symmetrical
except for a variation on the bottommost element; it rises
nobly from its base and manages to suggest a whole figure
while representing only the head and neck.

MLLE. POGANY III

Marble, 17 3/4" (45.1 cm.) high, 1931
Inscribed: C. Brancusi Paris 1931
Collection Philadelphia Museum of Art,
    The Louise and Walter Arensberg Collection; by bequest,
    1950
Provenance
Walter Arensberg, acquired 1932

Exhibitions
Art Institute of Chicago, 1949, no. 21
Philadelphia Museum, 1952, no. 15
Philadelphia Museum, 1954, no. 21, illus.
Guggenheim Museum, New York, 1955–56
    Philadelphia Museum, 1956

References
Geist no. 180

Philadelphia Museum Bulletin, March 1936, p. 2
Ritchie, 1952, p. 108
Read, 1956, p. 108
Zervos, 1957, p. 48
Giedion-Welcker, 1959, pl. 30
Jianou, 1963, pl. 30

Dated by the Arensbergs, for whom it was made.

In this final version of a theme first essayed in 1912 there
are several clear changes in design from the previous version: the two arms have given place to one arm; the hand
does not extend beyond the eyebrow; the eyelid sweeps
forward to the tip of the nose; the stepped areas of the
chignon continue to the bottom of the neck. These small
differences—which amount to the elimination of half-notes,
duplication and unresolved spaces—make for a design of
great purity and lightness.

PORTRAIT OF NANCY CUNARD

Polished bronze, 21 3/4" (55.2 cm.) high, 1932
Inscribed: C. Brancusi [and again] PAR C Brancusi 1932
               PARIS 1928
Collection Mr. and Mrs. Frederick Stafford, New York;
  acquired 1956 from the artist

Exhibitions
Brummer Gallery, New York, 1933–34, no. 26
Guggenheim Museum, New York, 1955–56
  Philadelphia Museum, 1956
World House Galleries, New York, 1957, no. 9
Staempfli Gallery, New York, 1960, no. 13, illus.
Isaac Delgado Museum of Art, New Orleans, 1966–67,
  no. 219, illus.

References
Geist no. 181
Zervos, 1957, p. 78
Giedion-Welcker, 1959, pl. 52
Jianou, 1963, pl. 59

The two dates in the inscription (on the bottom of the
bronze) are interpreted here as refering to the completion of
the plaster and to the casting of the work in bronze.

Aside from the absolute drawing of surfaces that high
polish demands, Brancusi has made a number of changes
from the wooden version that metal permits: the meeting
between head and neck is fine, the bottom of the neck
advances sharply, making an edge too fragile for wood,
and the neck itself is slightly longer. The head is less deep
and, most noticeably, the chignon is closer to the vertical.
The angle of the chignon is related to the more taut profile
of the face, a relation carried over from the original.

  In this bronze version we see Brancusi finding, as usual,
a reason for each change.

BLOND NEGRESS II

Polished bronze, 15 7/8" (40.3 cm.) high, 1933
Inscribed: C Brancusi [and] Brancusi
Collection Mrs. Barnett Malbin, Birmingham, Michigan
  (The Lydia and Harry Lewis Winston Collection);
  acquired November 10, 1952 from the artist

Exhibitions
University of Michigan, Ann Arbor, 1955, no. 9
Detroit Institute of Arts, 1957, no. 22, illus.
  Virginia Museum of Art, Richmond, 1957–58
  San Francisco Museum of Art, 1958
Museum of Art, Toledo, Ohio, 1960

References
Geist no. 182b
Degand and Arp, December 1957, p. 30
Winston, March 1958, p. 11
Giedion-Welcker, 1959, pl. 19
Seuphor, 1959, p. 60

Dated by the cast in the collection of The Museum of
Modern Art, New York.

The bronze after the marble *White Negress II* is the latest
evidence that in every version of this theme Brancusi,
defying expectation, can carry the perfections of the
previous version to a more advanced state.

MLLE. POGANY III

Polished bronze, 17 1/2″ (44.5 cm.) high, 1933
Inscribed: BRANCUSI PARIS 1933
Collection Mrs. John Wintersteen, Philadelphia

Exhibitions
Guggenheim Museum, New York, 1955–56
   Philadelphia Museum, 1956

References
Geist no. 183b
Jianou, 1963, pl. 32

Another cast is in the Musée d'Art Moderne, Paris.

To Malvina Hoffman, the American sculptor, Brancusi said of this bronze, "Perhaps I may think of a still better interpretation some day. Who can ever say that a work of art is finished." But this was his last *Mlle. Pogany*. It is a dazzling confection, a display of metallic design that verges on pure abstraction while still imprinted with the character of its early inspiration and the force of Brancusi's sentiment.

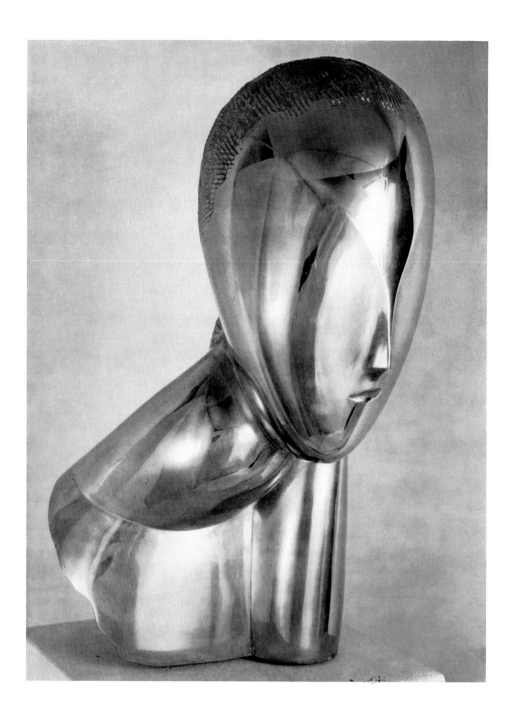

A MUSE

Polished bronze, 17 3/8″ (44.2 cm.) high, after 1918
Inscribed: C. BRANCUSI
Herbert and Nannette Rotschild Collection, Ossining,
    New York; acquired 1952 from the artist

Exhibitions
Museum of Art, Rhode Island School of Design,
    Providence, 1966, no. 16, illus.

References
Geist no. 104
Guilbert, 1957
Chelimsky, 1958, p. 18

In a final bronze of *A Muse* which Brancusi insisted to its
present owners should be known as *The Muse* (indicating
that the earlier title had come about by error) Brancusi cuts
the metal down to the height of the original marble. Unlike
the marble, the head of *The Muse* overhangs its base, the
shortened arm shows no unfinished areas, and the back has
been removed so that the hollow interior of the cast is
apparent.

THE COCK

Polished bronze, 40 3/4" (103.4 cm.) high, 1935
Inscribed: C. Brancusi 1935
Collection Musée National d'Art Moderne, Paris; acquired
   1946 from the artist

Exhibitions
Galerie Maeght, Paris, 1949
Kunsthaus, Zurich, 1954, no. 37
Guggenheim Museum, New York, 1955–56;
   Philadelphia Museum, 1956
Salon de Mai, Paris, 1957
Museum am Ostwall, Dortmund, 1959, no. 28, pl. 28
Orangerie, Kassel, 1959, no. 3, illus. p. 22
Charleroi, 1959–60
Museum Fridericianum, Kassel, 1964, no. 3, illus. p. 16
Athens, 1965
Expo 67, Montreal, 1967

References
Geist no. 187
Trier, 1954, pl. 66
Lewis, 1957, pls. 1, 57, 58
Zervos, 1957, p. 79
Giedion-Welcker, 1959, pls. 70, 71
Seuphor, 1960, p. 61

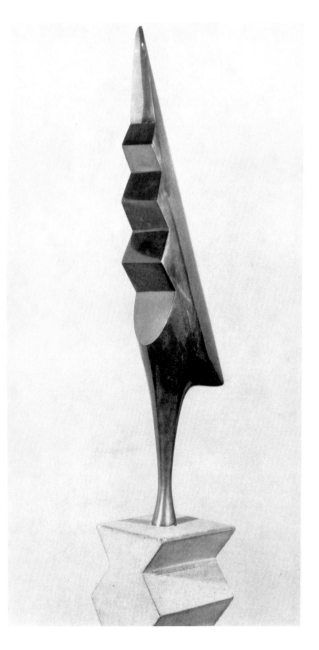

Over a period of twenty-seven years Brancusi worked on
possibly nine versions of this theme which culminated in the
sixteen-foot *Grand Coq*, plaster, of 1949. The earliest
version, in wood and titled *Coq Gaulois* by the sculptor, has
disappeared; it is known only by a photograph in the
Brancusi Bequest at the Musée d'Art Moderne, Paris (the
sculptor sent a copy to John Quinn). The work appears to
be completely fashioned; its surface has not been finished.
The general design is like that of the existing versions, but
it has a round body and distinct leg (which show it to
derive from the *Bird*) and four serrations rather than three.

Brancusi worked on a large-perhaps six-foot-tall version
in clay in 1923 (*This Quarter*, 1925, pl. 12). It differs from
the previous example in wood mainly in having three
serrations, a feature which henceforth will be permanent; no
cast is known.

In 1924 Brancusi carved a second *Cock* in wood (coll.
The Museum of Modern Art, New York) which was the
basis of all later variations.

By 1933 there were three monumental versions in plaster,
ranging in height from eight and a half to twelve feet. They
are relatively taller than the wood, as Brancusi compressed
the motif to columnar scope.

The Cock in bronze, though intimate in scale, pursues
this elongation. The brilliant, precisely rendered object
concentrates the special qualities of Brancusi's sculptural
intelligence—elegance, wit, rationality—in an incisive image
of unusual yet universally intelligible fantasy.

Grand Coq, *clay, 1923, destroyed* (left)

The Cock, *wood, 1924, coll. The Museum of Modern Art,*
   New York (right)

THE SEAL (MIRACLE)

Marble, 42 3/4″ × 44 7/8″ × 13″
  (108.6 × 114.0 × 33.0 cm.), 1936
Not inscribed
Collection The Solomon R. Guggenheim Museum, New York;
  acquired 1956 from the artist

Exhibitions
Museum of Modern Art, New York, 1939, no. 316, pl. 316
Philadelphia Museum, 1940, no. 47
Philadelphia Museum, 1952
  Art Institute of Chicago, 1953, no. 17
  Museum of Modern Art, New York, 1953, no. 17
Guggenheim Museum, New York, 1955–56

References
Geist no. 188
Giedion-Welcker, 1937, p. 104
Casson, 1939, p. 129
Zervos, 1957, p. 81
Giedion-Welcker, 1959, pls. 54 ?, 56
Jianou, 1963, pl. 60

The work was published in 1937 in *Moderne Kunst* by
Carola Giedion-Welcker, where it is dated 1936; there is
another version in marble in the Musée d'Art Moderne,
Paris. It has the alternate title: *The Miracle*.

The large design of *The Seal* resembles that of *Leda:* both
have the same bent axis; both show, at the bottom, a heavy
mass tapered at one end. *Leda* and *The Seal* are, besides,
the only sculptures of Brancusi set on bases that could be
turned by concealed motors. The resemblance ends there,
for whereas *Leda* shows two forms joined, *The Seal* is a
unitary form whose continuous roundness is accented only
by the plane at its upper end. With a great part of its mass
hovering over the base in an extension that advances as it
rises, *The Seal* is a subtle and precarious image whose
ambiguity reflects that of its natural model, a legless mam-
mal with fishy powers.

   This fluid form is stabilized with typical Brancusian rigor:
the plane of the face and the invisible plane of symmetry are
at a right angle to the base and to each other.

BIRD IN SPACE

Polished bronze, 53 3/8″ (135 cm.) high, 1940
Collection Peggy Guggenheim Foundation, Venice;
    acquired 1940 from the artist

Exhibitions
Art of This Century Gallery, New York, 1942, illus. p. 37
XXIV Biennale di Venezia, 1948, no. 13
Palazzo Venier dei Leoni, Venice, 1949, no. 3
Palais des Beaux-Arts, Brussels, 1951, no. 17
    Stedelijk Museum, Amsterdam, 1951, no. 17
Tate Gallery, London, 1964–65, no. 44, illus. p. 37
Guggenheim Museum, New York, 1969, illus. p. 32

References
Geis no. 196
Guggenheim, 1942, p. 37
Read, 1956, pl. 197
Lewis, 1957, 59a, b
Zervos, 1957, p. 85
Giedion-Welcker, 1959, pls. 62, 63
Guggenheim, 1960, pp. 71, 73
Jianou, 1963, pls. 49, 50
Calas, N. and E., 1966, no. 61
de Micheli, 1966, pl. VII

Dated by the statement of Miss Guggenheim; Zervos, 1957,
    p. 89

Although the Arensberg marble of 1924 may have been the
first version of the definitive design of *Bird in Space*, its
broken footing leaves the matter in doubt. The work in the
collection of the Kunsthaus, Zurich, is thus the first clear
example of this design; it was carved in 1925; the body and
footing are not continuous, but joined. In the sixteen years
that followed, Brancusi carved four other versions in marble,
all about six feet in height, each of which gave rise to a
bronze.

There are four variations in bronze from the Zurich
marble; the Peggy Guggenheim *Bird in Space* is the last of
these. While their heights remain in the neighborhood of
fifty-three inches, changes in other dimensions bring about
changes in proportion and total character. The present
Bird in Space is the slenderest of all versions in this size.

After the initial standing bird, the subsequent stretching
birds, and the later birds that seem to flow upward from
their bases, *Bird in Space*, with its undulating footing,
suggests full soaring flight. But not of any bird in nature.
It makes an image of spiritual flight, at once the nocturnal
and euphoric flight of erotic dream and the flight of the soul
in its urge to transcendence.

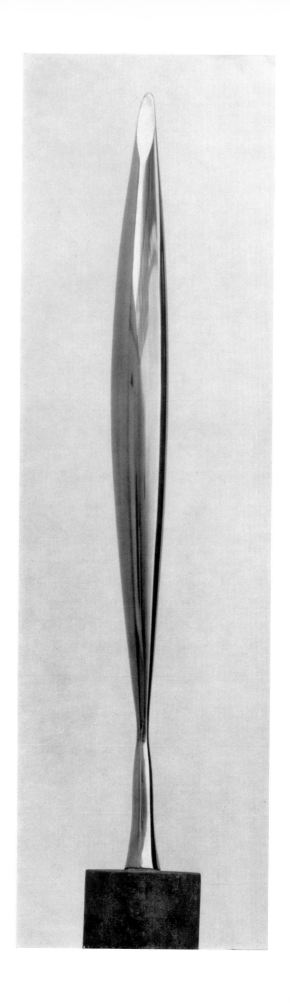

FLYING TURTLE

Marble, 12 1/2″ × 36 5/8″ × 27 1/8″
  (31.8 × 93.0 × 69.0 cm.), 1940–1945?
Not inscribed
Collection The Solomon R. Guggenheim Museum, New York;
  acquired 1956 from the artist

Exhibitions
Guggenheim Museum, New York, 1955–56
  Philadelphia Museum, 1956

References
Geist no. 201
Lewis, 1957, pls. 41, 42
Giedion-Welcker, 1959, pl. 73
Liberman, 1960, pl. 83
Jianou, 1963, pl. 61
De Micheli, 1966, pl. 2

The work appears in a roughed-out state in a photograph
probably made after the beginning of the second World War;
it was completed in the last year of the war, and first
photographed in 1946.

Flying Turtle is a variation of the wooden *Turtle* which
precedes it immediately. It is worth noting that while the
work is symmetrical in concept, like all of Brancusi's new
motifs after 1920, the tip of one foot is two inches (five
centimeters) further from the neck than the other.

Although *Flying Turtle* was followed by two works,
Boundary Marker and *Le Grand Coq IV*, we note that these
are variations on themes begun in 1907 and 1922. *Flying
Turtle* has a finality in the oeuvre which is triple: the turtle
is Brancusi's last new theme; *Flying Turtle* is the solution to
the sculptor's old problem of rendering relatively numerous
elements in a relatively unitary form; it is the last of a series
of works which explore spatial orientation, and as such has
a special significance, even poignance.

Bird in Space, rising vertically, is an image of the transcendence of the earthly; pointed upward, into a space
limitless on all sides, it has no need to face any particular
direction and so is essentially round. *Fish* suggests movement at a lower level parallel to the horizon and still free
from the earth. *The Turtle* is clearly oriented to the earth,
either crawling on it or planing above it. Extraordinarily,
Flying Turtle does neither of these things; placed at an
angle in unstable fashion, it suggests an unidentified object
in swooping flight. Given Brancusi's history there can be no
doubt that the work was originally conceived to be a sculpture of a turtle in its normal position, lying on the ventral
side, and so it was seen in Brancusi's studio by the writer
and by Constantin Antonovici, New York. One is led to
suppose that in turning the marble *Turtle* on its back
Brancusi was refusing at the last moment the logical out-
come of both his sculptural and spiritual progress. His
ascensional nature would have found the earth-hugging
image intolerable as a way to close the oeuvre. In overturning the *Turtle*, Brancusi asserts an intransigent humanity
against the pressures of reason and dream. *Flying Turtle* is
Brancusi's *défi* flung in the face of fate.

Turtle, *plaster cast of wood, 1943, coll. Musée National
d'Art Moderne, Paris*

Portrait of a Woman

While the sculpture of Brancusi shows an impressive consistency and continuity, the immediate feature of the graphic works is their unmethodical, unsystematic character, an impression reinforced by their small number, their variety of technique and the wide range of impulses that gave rise to them. It is, indeed, almost impossible to identify with certainty his drawings in a sketch-book left in Bucharest as he set out for Paris (aet. 27), since not only does the book contain drawings by other hands, but those that might be attributable to him have no recognizable style. Even his concentration on the task varies greatly: certain works are constructed with obvious care, in others the lines seem to wander over the page without control. Brancusi usually sets his subject centrally on the page where it occupies the space easily; yet the off-center *Nude* (coll. Guggenheim Museum) engages the whole sheet, as of course the drawings of the studio do. But Brancusi's touch, whether with pencil, pen or brush, is never monotonous or mechanical; one senses the hand and its movement.

Brancusi seems to have had no habit of drawing. He may have been put off by the virtual impossibility of achieving in a drawing the kind of absoluteness and precision of form that he arrived at after much labor in a sculpture. He was not a spontaneous artist and he mistrusted chance effects, yet the drawings are inevitably spontaneous. Rationality may inform the sculptures; an undisguised lyricism pervades the drawings.

They are for the most part a sheer indulgence in beauty—the beauty of women and children, and of the lines, marks and designs that the graphic gesture may produce. Thus he most often drew for his pleasure, at the same time that his pleasure was an act of homage. Few studies for other purposes; the drawings of hands (coll. Baer) may be those he made from Margit Pogany with the future portrait in mind.

Drawings or projects for sculpture are remarkably scarce (I once wrongly contested this point with the English critic, David Lewis); on the other hand there are numerous drawings *from* the sculpture once it was made, another evidence of Brancusi's realism. For the purpose of identification he included a beautiful small sketch of *A Muse* in a letter to John Quinn in 1917. When (in order to justify his prices) he wrote Quinn in 1920, "all these works are conceived directly in the material," we may take him to mean that he not only had not made clay studies of the works in question, he had not made drawings either; and none exist.

One sculpture, however, *for* which he seems to have made studies is *The First Step;* four are known (three of which are in the exhibition) and the attitude of the figure differs from the sculpture in such a way as to suggest they were done before and not after the carving. A sheet of ink drawings at the Musée d'Art Moderne shows Brancusi attempting to find the design of the lintel and columns of a Gate; a drawing of an early *Coq* may have been made to determine the position of the armature.

If Brancusi drew from his sculpture, some of his most beautiful drawings and gouaches are views of his work and materials scattered about his studio. It is a surprise to learn that a gouache showing him working at the forge was done from a photograph. When he invents or draws without a model, the fact is usually apparent, as in the fanciful illustrations for a volume of poetry by Ilirie Voronca, or the page called *Study for "The Princess"* in the exhibition. While the drawings of women are all design, all curves and curls and swirls, the portraits of Joyce done in April 1929 are observed sharply and without sentiment, though the touch is tender. On the other hand a drawing of Joyce composed of a spiral and three vertical lines and used as the frontispiece for Joyce's *Tales Told of Shem and Shaun,* is unique in the oeuvre in its abstraction; and Brancusi had ambivalent attitudes about it. He contributed drawings to *transatlantic review* and *This Quarter.* A poster for a "Bal Banal" in 1924 bore drawings by Brancusi and Picasso; Brancusi's contribution showed a nude child. On another drawing of a child he wrote the words, "*Quand nous ne sommes plus enfants nous sommes déjà morts.*"

Two drawings in the exhibition (coll. University of Nebraska and coll. Avnet), done from the same model and

Mlle. Pogany

surely on the same day, form a progression such as is often evident in the sculpture. The first is quite naturalistic, tentative and searching. On the second a strong and simple schema has been imposed without, surprisingly, disturbing the impression of faithfulness in the representation. In a typical Brancusian linking of extremes, this drawing is disposed around a rigid framework and yet has eyes that are almost alive.

The drawings, in the end, reflect many of the characteristics of the sculpture. They exhibit the same tendency to elision: in two self-portraits at the Musée d'Art Moderne the eye is lacking in a profile, the nose is absent in a full-face rendering. The generosity of the paper size, as in *Nude* and *The First Step* (Hirshhorn coll. and Musée d'Art Moderne), is typically Brancusian as is the largeness of form. The Guggenheim drawing and the virtuoso *Pogany* study (coll. Philadelphia Museum) reflect the gestural character of the sculpture. Brancusi's tact is evident in the frequent use of brown and off-white papers which have the effect of reducing contrast. His usually gentle images are interspersed with surprisingly incisive ones.

"There are too many lives," said Brancusi,[1] and he did not add greatly to their sum. Yet his drawings always engage the attention. Their diversity is that of a quick mind reacting to the present occasion with wit, grace and largesse.

S. G.

[1] Robert Payne, "Constantin Brancusi," *World Review,* October 1949, p. 63.

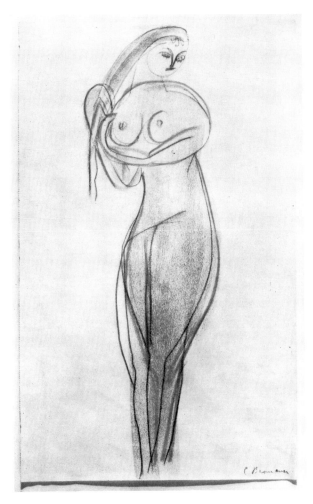

Study for "The Princess"

HEAD OF A GIRL
Charcoal, 16 1/4″ × 10 3/4″, ca. 1910
Collection Mr. and Mrs. Lester Francis Avnet, New York

* MLLE. POGANY
Charcoal on brown paper, 22 3/8″ × 16 1/8″, ca. 1912
Collection Philadelphia Museum of Art, A. E. Gallatin
    Collection

THE FIRST STEP
Pencil, 28 1/2″ × 12 1/8″, 1913
Joseph H. Hirshhorn Collection, New York

THE FIRST STEP
Charcoal on paper mounted on board, 29 1/4″ × 15″,
    ca. 1913
Collection Musée National d'Art Moderne, Paris

THE FIRST STEP
Pencil, 28 3/4 × 15″, ca. 1913
Joseph H. Hirshhorn Collection, New York

* Illustrated

Hands

* STUDY FOR "THE PRINCESS"
  Pencil and crayon on paper, 17" × 10 3/8", ca. 1913–15
  Collection Philadelphia Museum of Art, The Louise and
  Walter Arensberg Collection

STUDY FOR "THE NEWBORN"
Pencil and gouache on beige paper, 14 3/4" × 21 3/4",
1914
Collection Philadelphia Museum of Art, The Louise and
Walter Arensberg Collection

RECLINING HEAD ("THE FIRST CRY")
Gouache, 15" × 21", 1915
Joseph H. Hirshhorn Collection, New York

* PORTRAIT OF A WOMAN
  Oil on canvas, 24 1/8" × 15 5/8", ca. 1918
  Collection Mr. and Mrs. Lester Francis Avnet, New York

* VIEW OF THE STUDIO
  Gouache on board, 12 3/4" × 16 1/8", 1918
  Collection Mr. and Mrs. Lester Francis Avnet, New York

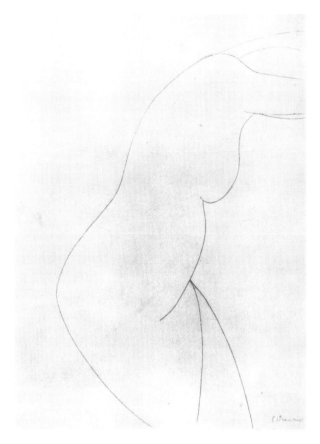

Nude

THE STUDIO
Pen and ink, 16 1/2″ × 12 1/2″, ca. 1920
Collection Mr. and Mrs. Lester Francis Avnet, New York

PORTRAIT OF JAMES JOYCE
Ink, 8″ × 6 7/8″, 1929
Private Collection

BIRDS IN THE SKY
Watercolor and gouache on paper, 12 1/8″ × 25 7/8″
Collection Musée National d'Art Moderne, Paris

MME. FRACHON
Pencil on rough brown paper, 25″ × 18 3/4″
Collection Mrs. Howard M. Kinney, Washington, D.C.

* HANDS
Pencil, 16 1/8″ × 21 1/8″
Collection Kathi Baer

HEAD OF A GIRL
Pencil on cardboard, 23″ × 15 3/8″
F. M. Hall Collection, University of Nebraska, Lincoln

Three Infants

HEAD OF A WOMAN
Pen and red ink on paper mounted on board, 17″ × 10 3/4″
Collection The Art Institute of Chicago, Gift of Mrs. C. J.
    Bulliet and Jack Bulliet In Memory of C. J. Bulliet

* NUDE
Pencil on board, 24 3/4″ × 18″
Collection The Solomon R. Guggenheim Museum, New York

NUDE (STUDY FOR FRESCO)
Gouache, 25 5/8″ × 18 1/8″
Collection R. Sturgis Ingersoll, Penllyn, Pennsylvania

NUDE
Watercolor and pencil, 10 1/8″ × 8 1/4″
Collection Mr. and Mrs. Adolf Schaap, Philadelphia

* THREE INFANTS
Pen and India ink on board, 18 1/2″ × 12 1/2″
Collection The Art Institute of Chicago, Gift of Robert Allerton

TORSO
Blue chalk on paper, 20″ × 12 1/4″
Collection The Metropolitan Museum of Art, New York,
    The Alfred Stieglitz Collection, 1949

UNTITLED
Ink, 14 3/8″ × 14 1/4″
Collection Mrs. Benjamin P. Watson, Danbury, Connecticut

View of the Studio

Chronology

1876   Born, February 19, in Hobitza, district of Gorj, Rumania, a farming village in the foothills of the Transylvanian Mountains.

1887   Runs away home; goes to Tirgu Jiu where he works in a dramshop.

1892   Goes to Craiova.

1895   Enters the Craiova School of Arts and Crafts.

1898   Is graduated with honors from Craiova School of Arts and Crafts; certificate dated September 28. Goes to Bucharest; enrolls in School of Fine Arts.

1901   Completes course at Bucharest School of Fine Arts. Takes a trip to Vienna, works in a factory for a brief period.

1902   Diploma from Bucharest School of Fine Arts, dated September 24.

1903   Does a commissioned portrait of Gen. Dr. Davila, a pioneer of Rumanian medicine. Leaves for Paris on foot.

1904   Arrives in Paris in the summer, having walked most of the way, and passed through Munich and Basel. Supports himself by washing dishes in a restaurant, and working and singing in a Ruminain church. Lives for a while at 9 Cité Condorcet.

1905   Lives at 10 Place de la Bourse. Enrolls at the École des Beaux-Arts, June 23, in the atelier of Antonin Mercié. Moves to 16 Place Dauphine.

1906   Exhibits at the Salon d'Antonine where he meets Rodin. Work acquired by Victor N. Popp.

1907   Leaves the École des Beaux-Arts. Possibly works for Rodin, end of March or early April. On April 18 gets a commission for a funerary monument in Rumania. Takes a studio at 54 rue du Montparnasse.

1908   Exhibits in Bucharest. Friendships with Rousseau, Matisse, Léger. Visit to Salon d'Aviation with Léger and Duchamp, December.

1909   Visits Bucharest. In Livorno with Modigliani.

1910   Meets Margit Pogany. Work acquired by Anastasiu Simu. Death of Rousseau. *The Kiss* installed at Cimetière Montparnasse on the grave of Tatiana Rashewsky.

1912   Awarded a First Prize at the Salonul Oficial, Bucharest. Meets Epstein. Carves Apollinaire's poem on gravestone of Rousseau. Meets A. B. Davies, who buys a work in marble.

1913   Five works in the Armory Show, New York.

1914   First one-man show, eight works, at the Gallery of the Photo-Secession, New York; shipment paid for by Mrs. Eugene Meyer, Jr.; installation by Edward Steichen. Works acquired by Alfred Stieglitz, Mrs. Meyer, John Quinn.

1916   Refused for military service. Is installed at 8 Impasse Ronsin.

1918   In hospital with broken leg.

1919   September: death of Maria, his mother.

1920   *Princess X* withdrawn from Salon des Indépendants, but *Yellow Bird* has place of honor. Attends "Festival Dada." Death of Modigliani. *Endless Column* in garden of Steichen home, Voulangis.

1921   Meets John Quinn. Between May 25 and June 21, visits Milan, Naples, Rumania, Prague, Belgium. Friendship with Cocteau, Satie, Tzara, Picabia. Two-week trip to Corsica with Radiguet. Autumn: a Brancusi Number of *The Little Review* with an appreciation by Ezra Pound and twenty-four plates.

1922   Trip to Rumania—Sibiu, Hobitza, Craiova, Bucharest—with Miss Eileen Lane; worked on a project for a Gate in stone in his native region.

1923   Plays golf with Quinn and H. P. Roché, while Jeanne Robert Foster and Satie observe.

1924   *transatlantic review* publishes five drawings. Summer at St. Raphaël, where he builds a "Temple of the Crocodile" on the beach. Death of Quinn.

1925   *This Quarter* publishes forty-six plates, aphorisms and a tale by Brancusi. Death of Satie. To London, October.

1926   Visits New York, January–March, to attend second one-man exhibition, at the Wildenstein Galleries. Meets Stieglitz. The Penguin Club gives party in

Brancusi at his graduation from the Craiova School of Arts and Crafts, September, 1898

Brancusi's honor. Roché and Duchamp acquire the Brancusis in the Quinn collection. Visits Belgium, May. Visits New York, September–December, to attend third one-man show, at the Brummer Gallery, New York.

1927   Trial begins concerning the status of *Bird in Space* (coll. Mrs. E. Steichen) as a work of art or an object of manufacture; U.S. Customs Court, New York. New studio at 11 Impasse Ronsin.

1928   Decision in Brancusi's favor at U.S. Customs Court trial.

1929   Drawing of Joyce for frontispiece of *Tales Told of Shem and Shaun*.

1930   Visits Ruminia.

1933   Maharajah of India acquires bronze *Bird in Space;* commissions two in marble; discusses poject for a "Temple of Meditation" in India. Fourth one-man exhibition, Brummer Gallery, New York.

1935   Invited to design a war memorial for Tirgu Jiu.

1937   On the jury of the Prix Helena Rubinstein. Visits Rumania, June–September, to work on war memorial. Returns to Tirgu Jiu, early November, to observe beginning of erection of *Endless Column*. Goes to India to work on "Temple of Meditation,"

but does not see the Maharajah; polishes his marble *Birds in Space*.

1938   Visits Egypt, January; then to Holland. Visits Rumania, summer, to work at Tirgu Jiu. Visits Rumania, autumn, for inauguration of ensemble at Tirgu Jiu.

1939   Visits New York, May–June, for the tenth anniversary of The Museum of Modern Art.

1945   Petre Pandrea, *Portrete si Controverse*, Bucharest; contains an 80-page study of Brancusi.

1947   V. G. Paleolog, *Brancusi*, Bucharest, the latest and most considerable of his three monographs on the sculptor.

1949   Completes *Grand Coq*, plaster, sixteen feet, his last work.

1955   Retrospective exhibition at The Solomon R. Guggenheim Museum, New York. Falls and breaks hip.

1956   80th Anniversary exhibition at the Muzeul de Arta R. S. R., Bucharest. Wills his studio and its contents to the Musée National d'Art Moderne, Paris. Becomes a French citizen. *Cahiers d'Art* publishes a ninety-one page article on Brancusi.

1957   Dies, March 16. Buried in Cimetière Montparnasse.

Brancusi, shortly after his arrival in Paris, ca. 1905

Portrait of Brancusi. *Amedeo Modigliani. Black and red pencil on brown paper, 20 1/8″ × 15 1/4″, ca. 1909. Lent to the exhibition by Mrs. Howard M. Kinney, Washington, D.C.*

Brancusi at Voulangis, ca. 1922. Photograph by Edward Steichen, coll. The Museum of Modern Art, New York

Documentation

ONE-MAN EXHIBITIONS

1914   March 12–April 1
Gallery of the Photo-Secession, New York

1926   February 21–March 3
Wildenstein Galleries, New York

November 17–December 15
Brummer Gallery, New York

Traveled to
January 4–18, 1927
The Arts Club of Chicago

1933   November 17, 1933–January 13, 1934
Brummer Gallery, New York

1955   October 25, 1955–January 8, 1956
The Solomon R. Guggenheim Museum, New York
A retrospective exhibition

Traveled to
January 27–February 26, 1956
Philadelphia Museum of Art

1956   December 1956–January 1957
Muzeul de Arta R. S. R., Bucharest
A retrospective exhibition on the occasion of the
80th birthday of the artist

1960   November 29–December 31
Staempfli Gallery, New York

GROUP EXHIBITIONS

1903 Palatul Ateneului, Bucharest

1906 April 15–June 30
Grand Palais, Paris
"Société Nationale des Beaux-Arts," XVI exp.

October 6–November 15
Grand Palais, Paris
"Société du Salon d'Automne," 4me exp.

1907 March 15–May 1
Bucharest
"6h Tinerimea Artistica"

April 14–June 30
Grand Palais, Paris
"Société Nationale des Beaux-Arts," XVII exp.

Summer
L'Abbaye de Créteil, France

October 1–22
Grand Palais, Paris
"Société du Salon d'Automne," 5me exp.

1908 March 9–May 1
Bucharest
"7h Tinerimea Artistica"

April 15–June 30
Grand Palais, Paris
"Société Nationale des Beaux-Arts," XVIII exp.

1909 March 15–April 15
Bucharest
"8h Tinerimea Artistica"

Bucharest
"Expozitia Oficiala"

October 1–November 8
Grand Palais, Paris
"Société du Salon d'Automne," 7me exp.

1910 March 18–May 1
Cours la Reine, Paris
"Société des Artistes Indépendants," (26me)

April 11–?
Bucharest
"9h Tinerimea Artistica"

November 10–?
Bucharest
"Autumn Exhibition of Tinerimea Artistica"

1911 April 21–June 13
Quai d'Orsay, Paris
"Société des Artistes Indépendants," (27me)

1912 Bucharest
"Salonul Oficial"

March 20–May 16
Quai d'Orsay, Paris
"Société des Artistes Indépendants," (28me)

1913 February 15–March 15
The Armory of the 69th Infantry, New York
"International exhibition of Modern Art" (The Armory Show)

Traveled to
March 24–April 16
The Art Institute of Chicago

April 28–May 19
Copley Society of Boston, Copley Hall

March 19–May 18
Quai d'Orsay, Paris
"Société des Artistes Indépendants," (29me)

March 31–?
Bucharest
"13h Tinerimea Artistica"

July
Albert Hall, London
"Allied Artists Exhibition"

1914 February–March
U. Praze Moderni Umeni, Prague
"Modern French Artists"

March 30–?
Bucharest
"14h Tinerimea Artistica"

1917 April 10–May 6
Grand Central Palace, New York
"Society of Independent Artists"

December 5–?
Hotel Ritz-Carlton, New York
"Allies of Sculpture"

1920 January 28–February 29
Grand Palais des Champs-Elysées, Paris
"Société des Artistes Indépendants," (31me)

March 21–?
Bucharest
"3rd Exhibition of Arta Romana"

April 30–June 15
Société Anonyme, New York
"First Exhibition"

August 2–September 11
Société Anonyme, New York
"Third Exhibition"

1922 March 24–April 16
Sculptors' Gallery, New York
"Contemporary French Art"

September 19–October 22
The Art Institute of Chicago
"The Arthur Jerome Eddy Collection"

1923 May 21–June 9
American Art Association, New York
"Spring Salon"

1924 November 30–December 30
Bucharest
1st International Exhibition, "Contimporanul"

1925 October
New Chenil Galleries, London
"Exhibition of Tri-National Art"

1926 January 7–30
The Art Center, New York
"John Quinn Collection / Memorial Exhibition of
    Representative Works"

January 26–February 17
Wildenstein Galleries, New York
"Tri-National Exhibition of Contemporary Art"

March 20–May 2
Palais de Bois, Paris
"Société des Artistes Indépendants," (37me)

June
Palais de Bois, Paris
"Salon des Tuileries"

November 19, 1926–January 1, 1927
The Brooklyn Museum, New York
"International Exhibition of Modern Art,"
    (43rd Société Anonyme)

1927 Galerie Jacques Bernheim, Paris
"Première Exposition Annuelle d'une Groupe de
    Sculpteurs"

April 1–24
Art Gallery of Toronto
"International Exhibition of Modern Art"

June
Palais de Bois, Paris
"Salon des Tuileries"

September 30–October 10
Bucharest
"Exposition d'Art Roumain – Congrès de la Presse
    Latine"

December 12–?
Museum of Living Art, New York University
"The A. E. Gallatin Collection"

1928 Bucharest
"8h Arta Romana"

Philadelphia Museum of Art
"Inaugural Exhibition"

May–June
Museum of Modern Art, Moscow
"Contemporary French Art"

June
Palais De Bois, Paris
"Salon des Tuileries"

October 26–?
Bucharest
"25h Anniversary of Tinerimea Artistica"

1929 Bucharest
"Black & White," Drawing and Print Salon

April
Galerie Georges Bernheim, Paris
"2me Exposition Internationale de la Sculpture"

June
Palais des Expositions, Paris
"Salon des Tuileries"

October 6–November 3
Kunsthaus, Zurich
"Abstrakte und Surrealistische Malerei und Plastik"

1930 May 3–25
The Hague
"Tentoonstelling van Roomenske Kunst"

July 20–August 10
Galerie Giroux, Brussels
"Exposition d'Art Roumain Moderne"

November 10–27
Print Club of Philadelphia
"Contemporary French Drawings"

1931 December 22, 1931–January 17, 1932
The Art Institute of Chicago
"The Arthur Jerome Eddy Collection"

1933 April 28–?
Sociedade Pro-Arte Moderna, São Paulo

June
Neo-Parnasse, Paris
"Salon des Tuileries"

June 1–November 1
The Art Institute of Chicago
"A Century of Progress Exposition"

November
Philadelphia Museum of Art
"The Ingersoll Collection"

1934 La France Institute, New York
"Modern Drawings"

May 12–June 3
Palais des Beaux-Arts, Brussels
"Exposition Minotaure"

June 20–August 20
Renaissance Society, University of Chicago
"A Selection of Works by XXth Century Artists"

1935 April 3–May 3
Chambre Internationale des Experts d'Art
"Trois Synthèses Artistiques"

1936 January 3–31
Albright Art Gallery, Buffalo, New York
"Art of Today"

June 11–July 4
New Burlington Galleries, London
"International Surrealist Exhibition"

March 2–April 19
The Museum of Modern Art, New York
"Cubism and Abstract Art"

    Traveled to
    January 8–February 7, 1937
    Cleveland Museum of Art

1937 Exposition Internationale, Paris
"Rumanian Art"

February
Columbus Gallery of Fine Arts, Ohio
"Sculpture of Seven Civilizations"

July 30–October 31
Musée du Jeu de Paume, Paris
"Origines et Développement de l'Art International
    Indépendant"

November 4–December 5
Cleveland Museum of Art, Ohio
"Sculpture of Our Time"

1938 Summer
Gallery Guggenheim Jeune, London
"Contemporary Sculpture"

1939 May 10–September 30
The Museum of Modern Art, New York
"Art in Our Time"

1940 May 18–October 1
Philadelphia Museum of Art
"Sculpture International"

April 25–May 26
The Art Institute of Chicago
"International Exhibition of Watercolors"

1941 February 11–March 8
Buchholz Gallery, New York
"From Rodin to Brancusi"

1942 November 10–December 5
Buchholz Gallery, New York
"Homage to Rodin"

December 9, 1942–January 24, 1943
The Museum of Modern Art, New York
"20th Century Portraits"

1943 October 24–November 10
Craiova, Rumania
"The Week of Oltenia"

1944 March 18–April 16
Cincinnati Art Museum, Ohio
"Pictures for Peace"

March 29–May 17
Philadelphia Museum of Art
"History of an American: Alfred Stieglitz: '291' and
    After"

April 10–29
Valentine Gallery, New York
"The Lee Ault Collection"

1946 March 30–May 1
City Art Museum of St. Louis, Missouri
"Origins of Modern Sculpture"

October 1–November 15
Cincinnati Art Museum, Ohio
"4 Modern Sculptors"

October 24–December 1
Newark Museum, New Jersey
"Owned in New Jersey"

1947 June 10–August 31
The Museum of Modern Art, New York
"Alfred Stieglitz Memorial"

July 1–4
Club de Chaillot, Paris
"L'Art Français au Secours des Enfants Roumains"

December
Dum Umeni, Brno, Czechoslovakia
"French Sculptors from Rodin to Our Time"

1948   Stedelijk Museum, Amsterdam
       "13 Beeldhouwers uit Parijs"

       April 15–May 23
       Baltimore Museum of Art
       "Themes and Variations in Painting and Sculpture"

       June 4–September 8
       XXIV Biennale di Venezia
       "Peggy Guggenheim Collection"

       November 16, 1948–January 23, 1949
       The Museum of Modern Art, New York
       "Timeless Aspects of Modern Art"

1949   Minneapolis Institute of Arts, Minnesota
       "Masterpieces of Sculpture"

       January 14–February 13
       Yale University Art Gallery, New Haven
       "Sculpture Since Rodin"

       April 30–May 13
       Galerie Maeght, Paris
       "Préliminaires à l'Art Abstrait"

       September
       Palazzo Venier dei Leoni, Venice
       "Mostra di Sculptura Contemporanea"

       September 26–October 14
       Buchholz Gallery, New York
       "Sculpture"

       October 20–December 18
       The Art Institute of Chicago
       "20th Century Art from the Louise and Walter
          Arensberg Collection"

       November 29–December 17
       M. Knoedler & Co., Inc., New York
       "To Honor Henry McBride"

1950   February
       Philadelphia Museum of Art
       "The S. S. White Collection"

       March 30–May 18
       Museum of Art, Rhode Island School of Design,
          Providence
       "A Century of Sculpture, 1850–1950"

       May
       Philadelphia Museum of Art
       "Masterpieces of Philadelphia Private Collections"

       September 26–October 14
       Buchholz Gallery, New York
       "Contemporary Drawings"

       December 6, 1950–January 6, 1951
       Buchholz Gallery, New York
       "The Heritage of Auguste Rodin"

1951   Palais des Beaux-Arts, Brussels
       "Surréalisme + Abstraction," Collection Peggy
          Guggenheim

          Traveled to
          Stedelijk Museum, Amsterdam

July 6–September 25
Stedelijk Museum, Amsterdam
"De Stijl"

September 17–October 27
Sidney Janis Gallery, New York
"From Brancusi to Duchamp"

December
Desert School of Art, Scottsdale, Arizona
"Sculpture from Rodin to Today"

1952   February
       National Gallery of Victoria, Melbourne

       May–June
       Musée National d'Art Moderne, Paris
       "L'Oeuvre du XXe Siècle"

          Traveled to
          July 15–August 17
          Tate Gallery, London
          as "20th Century Masterpieces"

       October 11–December 7
       Philadelphia Museum of Art
       "Sculpture of the Twentieth Century"

          Traveled to
          January 22–March 8, 1953
          The Art Institute of Chicago

          April 29–September 7
          The Museum of Modern Art, New York

       December 15, 1952–February 1, 1953
       Yale University Art Gallery, New Haven, Connecticut
       "In Memory of Katherine S. Dreier, 1877–1952 –
          Her Own Collection of Modern Art"

1953   January 19–February 14
       Sidney Janis Gallery, New York
       "French Masters"

       January 30–April 9
       Musée National d'Art Moderne, Paris
       "Le Cubisme 1907–1914"

       June 20–September 30
       Parc Middelheim, Antwerp
       "2me Biennale de la Sculpture"

       November
       Museum of Fine Arts, Houston
       "75 Years of Sculpture"

       November 1953–February 1954
       Museum of Modern Art, São Paulo
       "II Bienal de São Paulo"

       December 22, 1953–January 24, 1954
       Curt Valentin Gallery, New York
       "Sculpture and Sculptor's Drawings"

1954   July 18–September 28
       Hôtel de Ville, Yverdon, Switzerland
       "Sept Pionniers de la Sculpture Moderne"

          Traveled to
          November 27–December 31
          Kunsthaus, Zurich
          as "Begründer der Modernen Plastik"

October 16
Philadelphia Museum of Art
Opening of "The Louise and Walter Arensberg
Collection"

1955   January 12–March 6
Cranbrook Academy of Art Galleries, Bloomfield
Hills, Michigan
"The Levin Collection"

June 8–?
Curt Valentin Gallery, New York
"Closing Exhibition: Sculpture, Paintings and
Drawings"

October 30–November 27
Museum of Art, University of Michigan, Ann Arbor
"20th Century Paintings and Sculpture from the
Winston Collection"

1956   October 9–November 3
Fine Arts Associates, New York
"Rodin to Lipchitz, Part II"

1957   January 14–February 8
M. Knoedler & Co., Inc., New York
"Minneapolis Institute of Arts Benefit"

January 22–February 23
World House Galleries, New York
"The Struggle for New Form"

February
Philadelphia Museum of Art
"The T. Edward Hanley Collection"

February 15–March 10
Society of the Four Arts, Palm Beach, Florida

March 28–April 20
World House Galleries, New York
"Four Masters: Rodin, Brancusi, Gauguin, Calder"

April 22–May 11
Sidney Janis Gallery, New York
"Brancusi to Giacometti"

July 27–November 4
Milan
"XI Trienalle di Milano"

September 27–November 3
Detroit Institute of Arts
"Collecting Modern Art: Paintings, Sculpture and
Drawings from the collection of Mr. and Mrs.
Harry Lewis Winston"

Traveled to
December 13, 1957–January 5, 1958
Virginia Museum of Art, Richmond

January 23–March 13, 1958
San Francisco Museum of Art

April 11–May 12, 1958
Milwaukee Art Institute

October 11–November 17
Museum of Fine Arts, Boston
"European Masters of Our Time"

1958   January 5–February 3
Amherst College, Amherst, Massachusetts
"45th Anniversary of the Armory Show"

April 17–October 19
Exposition Universelle de Bruxelles
"50 Ans d'Art Moderne"

Summer
World House Galleries, New York
"Summer International II"

September 25–November 9
Contemporary Arts Museum, Houston
"The Trojan Horse Exhibit of Art of the Machine"

September 29–November 1
Sidney Janis Gallery, New York
"10th Anniversary Exhibition"

1959   Belgrade
"Rumanian Art"

Traveled to
November
Budapest

March–April, 1960
Bratislava

May–June 1960
Prague

June–July 1960
East Berlin

Charleroi, Belgium
"De Maillol à nos Jours"

February 25–March 28
World House Galleries, New York
"Daumier to Picasso"

May–June
Museum am Ostwall, Dortmund
"Französische Plastik des 20. Jahrhunderts"

Summer
World House Galleries, New York
"Summer International III"

July 11–October 11
Orangerie, Kassel, Germany
"II. Documenta '59"

September 21–October 10
Fine Arts Associates, New York
"Sculpture and Sculptors' Drawings"

October 28–December 7
Dallas Museum for Contemporary Arts
"Signposts of 20th Century Art"

December 8, 1959–January 9, 1960
World House Galleries, New York
"Drawings, Watercolors and Collage by 20th Century
Masters"

1960   Musée d'Art et d'Industrie, St. Etienne, France
"Cent Sculptures de Daumier à nos jours"

March
Museum of Art, Toledo, Ohio
"What is Modern Art?"

March 6–April 3
University of California, Berkeley
"Art From Ingres to Pollock"

March 8–April 25
Musée Cantini, Marseille
"Sculpture Contemporaine"

March 25–September 25
Museum Boymans-van Beuningen, Rotterdam
"Beeldenstoonstelling Floriade"

April 12–May 14
M. Knoedler & Co., Inc., New York
"The Colin Collection"

April 19–May 19
The Arts Club of Chicago
"Sculpture and Drawings by Sculptors from the
    Solomon R. Guggenheim Museum"

May 8–June 6
William Rockhill Nelson Gallery of Art, Kansas City,
    Missouri
"Art and Anatomy"

May 19–June 26
Yale University Art Gallery, New Haven
"Paintings, Drawings and Sculpture Collected by
    Yale Alumni"

June 18–October 16
Venice
"XXX Biennale di Venezia"

June 22–July 29
World House Galleries, New York
"Summer International IV"

October 3–November 5
Sidney Janis Gallery, New York
"20th Century Artists"

October 4–November 13
Cleveland Museum of Art, Ohio
"Paths of Abstract Art"

1961   January 18–February 13
City Art Museum of St. Louis, Missouri
"A Galaxy of Treasures from St. Louis Collections"

February 10–?
Galerie Europe, Paris
"Klee Kandinsky Brancusi"

February 27–March 15
Palais des Beaux-Arts, Brussels
"Collection de M. et Mme. Burden"

April 5–30
Institute of Design, Chicago
"Maremont Collection"

June 11–August 25
Fogg Art Museum, Cambridge, Massachusetts
"Works of Art from the Collection of Harvard Class
    of 1936"

June 27–August 4
World House Galleries, New York
"Summer International"

July–September
Musée Rodin, Paris
"Exposition Internationale de Sculpture"

September
Svensk-Franska Konstgalleriet, Stockholm
"Fautrier – Brancusi"

October 25–December 4
Musée National d'Art Moderne, Paris
"L'Art Roumain du XIX Siècle à Nos Jours"

October 30–December 2
Sidney Janis Gallery, New York
"European Artists from A to V"

November 2, 1961–January 7, 1962
Philadelphia Museum of Art
"Guggenheim Museum Exhibition"

1962   Galerie de l'Institut, Paris
"Dessins de Sculpteurs"

January 2–20
Staempfli Gallery, New York
"Twenty Sculptors"

February 20–March 17
World House Galleries, New York
"Sculpture: Daumier to Picasso"

May 22–June
Galerie de l'Oeil, Paris
"Exposition Minotaure"

September 12–December 9
Wallraf-Richartz-Museum, Cologne
"Europäische Kunst 1912"

October 3, 1962–January 6, 1963
The Solomon R. Guggenheim Museum, New York
"Modern Sculpture from the Joseph Hirshhorn
    Collection"

1963   February 17–March 31
Munson-Williams-Proctor Institute, Utica, New York
"Armory Show: 50th Anniversary"

    Traveled to
    April 6–28
    69th Regiment Armory, New York

February 18–March 24
The Jewish Museum, New York
"The Hebrew Bible in Christian, Jewish and Muslim
    Art"

May 3–?
Portland Art Museum, Oregon
"Sculpture from West Coast Art Collectors"

May 15–June 8
M. Knoedler & Co., Inc., New York
"Reader's Digest Collection"

May 28–June 30
Künstlerhaus, Vienna
"Rumänische Malerei und Plastik: Ciucurencu,
    Brîncuşi, Caragea"

September 17–October 31
The Washington Gallery of Modern Art, Washington,
    D.C.
"Sculptors of Our Time"

October 3–November 17
Philadelphia Museum of Art
"Philadelphia Collects 20th Century Art"

1964 February 4–29
Sidney Janis Gallery, New York
"The Classic Spirit in 20th Century Art"

February 25–March 21
Staempfli Gallery, New York
"Stone Wood Metal"

February 28–March 28
Galerie Creuzevault, Paris

March 3–April 4
Sidney Janis Gallery, New York
"Two Generations: Picasso to Pollock"

May–September
Lausanne, Switzerland
"Exposition Nationale Suisse"

June 27–October 5
Museum Fridericianum, Kassel, Germany
"III. Documenta"

July 3–August 30
Museum des 20. Jahrhunderts, Vienna
"Meisterwerke der Plastik"

October 6–November 15
Baltimore Museum of Art
"1914: 50th Anniversary of the Baltimore Museum
of Art"

November 24–December 26
Sidney Janis Gallery, New York
"Three Generations"

December 31, 1964–March 7, 1965
Tate Gallery, London
"Peggy Guggenheim Collection"

1965 February 23–March 20
Staempfli Gallery, New York
"Stone and Crystal"

May 12–June 13
Dallas Museum of Fine Arts
"Sculpture of the 20th Century"

May–August
Recklinghausen, Germany
"Ruhrfestspiele"

September 8–November 8
Athens
"1st International Biennale of Sculpture"
(Panathenea of World Sculpture)

October 2–24
University of California, Irvine
"20th Century Sculpture, 1900–1950

October 21–December 8
Museum of Fine Arts, Houston
"The Heroic Years: Paris 1908–1914"

October 23–December 12
Wallraf-Richartz-Museum, Cologne
"Traum – Zeichen – Raum"

1966 January 6–February 20
Carpenter Center for Visual Arts, Harvard University,
Cambridge, Massachusetts
"Light and Color"

February 8–March 5
Sidney Janis Gallery, New York
"Old Masters in 20th Century Art"

March
Cleveland Museum of Art, Ohio
"Fifty Years of Modern Art"

April 26–May 21
M. Knoedler & Co., Inc., New York, and
Perls Galleries, New York
"Seven Decades: 1895–1965"

October 7–November 6
Museum of Art, Rhode Island School of Design,
Providence
"Herbert and Nannette Rothschild Collection"

October 26–November 26
Royal College of Art, London
"Rumanian art of the 20th century: Brancusi and his
countrymen"

November 11, 1966–January 8, 1967
Delgado Art Museum, New Orleans
"Odyssey of an Art Collector: Mr. and Mrs.
Frederick Stafford Collection"

1967 January 3–27
Sidney Janis Gallery, New York
"Two Generations of European and American Artists"

January 10–?
Galerie Claude Bernard, Paris
"Portraits"

April 28–October 27
Expo 67, Montreal
"Man and His World"

Summer
Musée du Jeu de Paume, Paris
"Chefs d'oeuvres des collections Suisses"

December 5–29
M. Knoedler & Co., Inc., New York
"Space and Dream"

1968 January 23–March 24
City Art Museum, St. Louis, Missouri
"'Works of Art of the Nienteenth and Twentieth
Centuries' collected by Louise and Joseph
Pulitzer, Jr."

March
Austin, Texas
"Governor's Conference on the Arts"

July
Grosvenor Galleries, London
"Twentieth Century Paintings and Sculpture"

1969 January 8–February 1
Sidney Janis Gallery
"20th Century Masters"

January 16–March 23
The Solomon R. Guggenheim Museum, New York
"Selections from the Peggy Guggenheim Collection"

A SELECTED BIBLIOGRAPHY

ADRIAN, P. G. "Brancusi," *Goya*, January 1957, pp. 235–240.

ALVARD, J. "L'Atelier de Brancusi," *Art d'Aujourd'hui*, January 1951, pp. 5, 8.

America & Alfred Stieglitz: A Collective Portrait, edited by Waldo Frank et al., New York, Doubleday, Doran and Co., 1934.

The American Magazine of Art, "Field Notes. Pennsylvania Museum Accessions," September 1933, p. 431.

The Art Digest, "1913–1933," September 1, 1933, p. 3.

The Art News, "Bird in Space, from the Collection of Stephen C. Clark," November 18, 1933, p. 1.

The Arts, vol. 2, no. 3, 1922.

BREZIANU, BARBU. "Le Secret du 'Baiser' de Brancusi," *La Revue du Louvre*, no. 1, 1969.

———. "Reportaj in jurul unei camere," *Secolul XX*, no. 11, 1967.

BURNHAM, JACK. *Beyond Modern Sculpture*, New York, George Braziller, Inc., 1968.

Cahiers d'Art, "Les Expositions à Paris et ailleurs," no. 10, 1927, p. 4.

Cahiers d'Art, nos. 1–4, 1935, p. 96.

CASSON, STANLEY. "Sculpture Today," *The Studio*, special spring issue, 1939.

CHELIMSKY, OSCAR. "A Memoir of Brancusi," *Arts*, June 1958, pp. 19–21.

The Chicago Art Institute Bulletin, 1936.

The Chicago Art Institute Bulletin, September 1949.

The Colin Collection, New York, M. Knoedler and Company, Inc., 1960.

DEGAND, LEO and ARP, JEAN. "La Collection H. et L. Winston au Musée de Detroit," *Aujourd'hui*, December 1957.

Dictionnaire de la Sculpture Moderne, Paris, Fernand Hazan, 1960.

DREIER, KATHERINE S. and DUCHAMP, MARCEL, eds., *Collection of the Société Anonyme*, New Haven, Yale University Art Gallery, 1950.

DREYFUS, ALBERT. "Constantin Brancusi," *Cahiers d'Art*, vol. 2, no. 2, 1927, pp. 69–74.

EDDY, ARTHUR JEROME. *Cubists and Post-Impressionism*, Chicago, A. C. McClurg, 1914.

EINSTEIN, CARL. *Die Kunst des 20. Jahrhunderts*, Berlin, Propyläen-Verlag, 1st edition, 1926; 3rd edition, 1931.

FIERENS, PAUL. *Sculpteurs d'aujourd'hui*, Chroniques du Jour, Paris, 1933.

———. "Brancusi," *Magazine of Art*, December 1949, pp. 290–295.

FOSTER, JEANNE ROBERT. "New Sculptures by Constantin Brancusi," *Vanity Fair*, May 1922, p. 68 ff.

GERTZ, ULRICH. *Plastik der Gegenwart*, Berlin, Rembrandt Verlag, 1953.

GEIST, SIDNEY. "Brancusi Catalogued?" [Review of Ionel Jianou, *Constantin Brancusi*], *Arts Magazine*, January 1964, pp. 63–73.

———. "Looking for Brancusi," *Arts Magazine*, October 1964, pp. 48–57.

———. *Brancusi, A Study of the Sculpture*, New York, Grossman Publishers, Inc., 1968.

———, and SPEAR, ATHENA TACHA. An exchange of letters, *The Art Bulletin*, September–December 1966, pp. 462–468.

GIEDION-WELCKER, CAROLA. *Moderne Plastik*, Zurich, Girsberger Verlag, 1937.

———. *Constantin Brancusi*, New York, George Braziller, Inc., 1959.

GINDERTAEL, R. V. "Brancusi l'inaccessible," *Cimaise*, January–February 1956, pp. 9–15.

GOLDWATER, ROBERT. "The Arensberg Collection for Philadelphia," *The Burlington Magazine*, November 1954, pp. 350–353.

———. *Space and Dream*, New York, Walker and Co. with M. Knoedler and Co., Inc., 1967, pp. 32–33.

GUÉGUEN, PIERRE. "La Sculpture cubiste," *Art d'aujourd'hui*, May–June 1953, pp. 50–58.

GUGGENHEIM, PEGGY, ed. *Art of this Century*, Art Aid Corporation, New York, 1942.

GUILBERT, CLAIRE GILLES. "Propos de Brancusi (1876–1957)," *Prisme des Arts*, no. 12, 1957, pp. 5–7.

HABASQUE, GUY. "L'Armory Show," *L'Oeil*, February 1959, pp. 10–18.

HAMILTON, GEORGE HEARD. "Anonyme no Longer," *Art News*, January 1953, p. 36.

———. *Painting and Sculpture in Europe. 1880–1940*. Harmondsworth, Middlesex, England, The Pelican History of Art, Penguin Books, Ltd., 1967.

HOFFMAN, MALVINA. *Sculpture Inside and Out*, New York, W. W. Norton and Co., 1939.

The J. B. Speed Art Museum Bulletin, "Mlle. Pogany by Brancusi," May 1955.

JIANOU, IONEL. *Brancusi*, New York, Tudor Publishing Co., 1963.

F. K. [FISKE KIMBALL]. "Opening of the Louise and Walter Arensberg Collection," *Philadelphia Museum Bulletin*, Autumn 1954, p. 7.

LANGUI, EMILE. *50 Years of Modern Art*, New York, Frederick A. Praeger, 1959.

LEWIS, DAVID. *Constantin Brancusi*, New York, Wittenborn, Inc., 1957.

LIBERMAN, ALEXANDER. *The Artist in His Studio*, New York, Viking Press, 1960.

LICHT, FRED. *A History of Western Sculpture: Sculpture 19th and 20th Centuries*, Greenwich, Connecticut, New York Graphic Society, 1967.

M. M. "Constantin Brancusi: A Summary of Many Conversations," *The Arts*, July 1923, pp. 15–29.

MARCHIORI, GIUSEPPI. *Modern French Sculpture*, New York, Harry N. Abrams, Inc., 1963.

MARTEL, JAN and JOEL. *Sculpture*, Paris, Moreau, 1929.

MARTIN, J. L., NICHOLSON, BEN and GABO, NAUM, eds., *Circle*, London, Faber and Faber, 1937.

MÉNIER, M. "Sculptures Recemment Acquises," *La Revue du Louvre*, no. 1, 1967, pp. 39–42.

DE MICHELI, MARIO. *Constantin Brancusi*, I Maestri della Scultura, no. 46, Milan, Fratelli Fabri, 1966.

NICOARĂ, MIRCEA. "Însemnări," *Familia*, February 1966.

OPREA, PETRE. "Constantin Brancusi: Données biographiques," *Cahiers d'Art*, vols. 33–35, 1960, pp. 189–196.

OZENFANT, AMÉDÉE. *Foundations of Modern Art*, Paris, Dover Publications, Inc., 1928.

PALEOLOG, V. G. *Brancusi*, Bucharest, 1947.

The Pennsylvania Museum Bulletin, no. 156, May 1933.

The Pennsylvania Museum Bulletin, no. 170, March 1936.

Philadelphia Museum of Art Bulletin, "The Samuel S. White, 3rd and Vera White Collection," January–March 1968 and April–June 1968, pp. 82–83.

Portland Art Association, "Sixty-seventh Annual Report," 1959, p. 2.

POUND, EZRA. "Brancusi," *The Little Review*, Autumn 1921, pp. 3–7.

———. "Über Zeitgenossen," Zurich, Die Arche, 1959.

READ, HERBERT. *The Art of Sculpture*, New York, Pantheon Books, 1956.

RINDGE, A. M. *Sculpture*, New York, Payson and Clarke Ltd., 1929.

RITCHIE, ANDREW CARDUFF. *Sculpture of the Twentieth Century*, New York, The Museum of Modern Art, 1952.

SĂNDULESCU, NICOLAE. *Brâncuși*, Bucharest, Meridiane Publishing House, 1965.

SCHAEFER-SIMMERN, HENRY. *Sculpture in Europe Today*, Berkeley, University of California Press, 1955.

SELZ, JEAN. *Modern Sculpture*, New York, George Braziller, 1963.

SEUPHOR, MICHEL. *L'Art Abstrait, Ses Origines, Ses Premiers Maîtres*, Paris, Maeght, 1949.

———. *La Sculpture de ce siècle*, Neuchâtel, Switzerland, Éditions du Griffon, 1959.

SOBY, JAMES THRALL. "The Arensberg Collection," *The Saturday Review*, November 6, 1954, pp. 60–61.

SPEAR, ATHENA TACHA. "A Contribution to Brancusi Chronology," *The Art Bulletin*, March 1966, pp. 45–49.

This Quarter, vol. 1, no. 1, 1925, 46 reproductions, aphorisms and tales by Brancusi [see appendix].

Transition, June 1929, p. 296 ff.

Transition, Fall 1936, p. 67.

TRIER, EDUARD. *Moderne Plastik*, Berlin, Verlag Gebr. Mama, 1954.

VALENTINER, W. R. *Origins of Modern Sculpture*, New York, Wittenborn and Co., 1946.

View, March–April 1946.

VITRAC, ROGER. "Constantin Brancusi," *Cahiers d'Art*, nos. 8–9, 1929, pp. 383–396.

WINSTON, HARRY and LYDIA K. "Collecting Modern Art," *Vassar Alumnae Magazine*, March 1958.

ZERVOS, CHRISTIAN. "Notes sur la Sculpture contemporaine," *Cahiers d'Art*, no. 10, 1929, pp. 465–473.

———. "Réflexions sur Brancusi: À propos de son exposition à New York," *Cahiers d'Art*, vol. 9, nos. 1–4, 1934, p. 80–83.

———. *Constantin Brancusi*, Paris, Cahiers d'Art, 1957.

ZORACH, WILLIAM. "The Sculpture of Constantin Brancusi," *The Arts*, March 1926, pp. 143–150.

The Brancusi illustrations—not numbered—which appear in
This Quarter, 1925, Paris, are listed here by their captions,
in the order in which they appear, and with our numbers.
Note that the date on number 42 is lacking the final numeral.

THIS QUARTER
[1] Brancusi. [2] La Danse. [3] Enfant. [4] Création.
[5] Devant la glace. [6] Croquis. [7] Brancusi jouant avec
Polaire. [8] Brancusi travaillant à la colonne sans fin.
[9] Vue d'atelier 1925. [10] L'oiseau blanc (inachevé).
[11] La colonne sans fin. [12] Le coq (projet pour bronze).
[13] Tors (plâtre). [14] La Sorcière. [15] Vue d'atelier,
1925. [16] La négresse blanche (albâtre). [17] Sculpture
(bois et pierre 1925). [18] Le chef (bois et fer 1924).
[19] Socrate (bois 1923). [20] Socrate (bois 1923].
[21] Mlle. Pogany. [22] Socrate et Platon (bois). [23] Le
Poisson (bronze poli, 1923). [24] Léda (marbre 1922).
[25] Eve (bois 1922). [26] Vue d'atelier. [27] L'oiseau
d'or, 1920. [28] Adam (bois 1921). [29] Eve (bois 1920).
[30] La Princesse X, 1917. [31] Le Baiser (cimetière Montparnasse). [32] Madame L. R. (bois 1916). [33] L'enfant
prodigue (bois 1914). [34] La muse endormie (marbre
1911). [35] La Baronne R. F. (pierre 1910). [36] Narcisse
(marbre 1909). [37] Narcisse (plâtre 1909). [38] Portrait
(marbre 1909). [39] Brancusi au golf. [40] La prière.
[41] La sagesse (pierre 1908). [42] Première pierre directe,
1900. [43] L'enfant (bronze 1907). [44] Portrait (1906).
[45] Ecorché. Modèle accepté a l'École de Médecine et des
Beaux-Arts, Roumanie, 1903. [46] Laocoon (copie). Premier
à l'École des Beaux-Arts de Bucarest.

Exhibition 69/8

8,500 copies of this catalogue designed by Arthur S. Congdon
have been printed by Brüder Rosenbaum, Vienna
in September 1969 for the Trustees of The Solomon R. Guggenheim Foundation
on the occasion of the loan exhibition
"Constantin Brancusi, 1876–1957: A Retrospective Exhibition."